Incredible bakes*

Incredible bakes*

*that just happen to
be refined-sugar free!

Caroline Griffiths

Smith
Street
Books

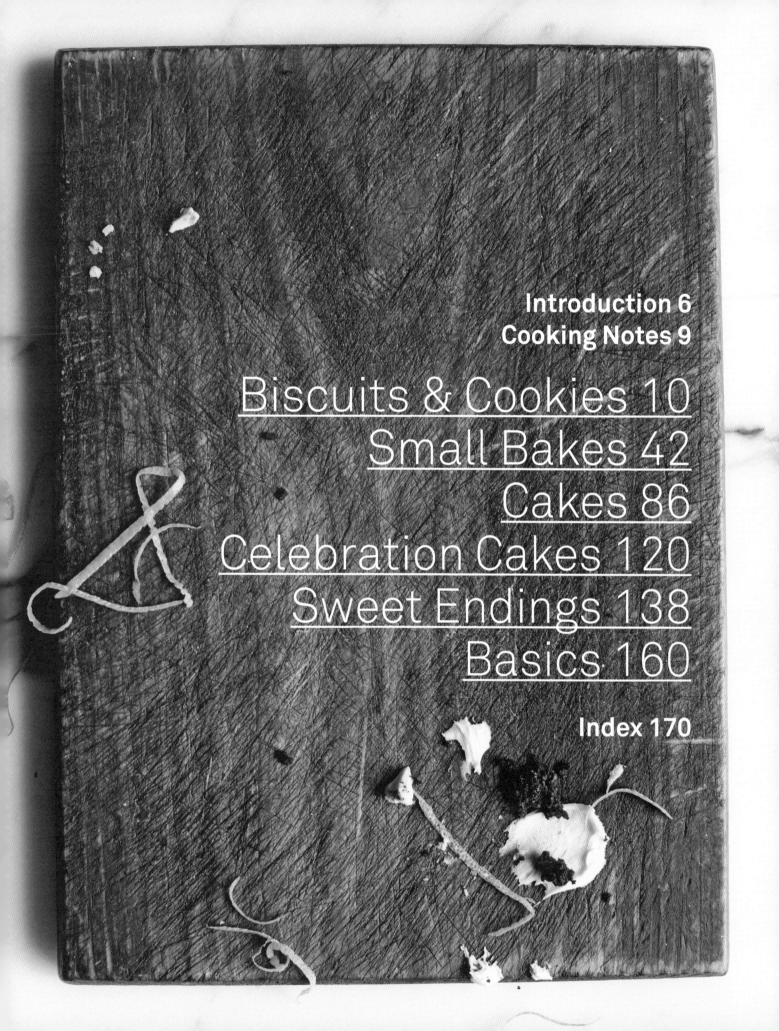

Introduction 6
Cooking Notes 9

Biscuits & Cookies 10
Small Bakes 42
Cakes 86
Celebration Cakes 120
Sweet Endings 138
Basics 160

Index 170

Introduction

Love baking? Me too. I enjoy the whole process and the buzz from the knowledge that I am making others happy with something I have created with love and care.

If that incredible bake just happens to be sugar-free or have less sugar than you would expect, then even better. More power to me. Without relying on sugar, the unique flavours of pure vanilla, nuts, spices and chocolate get their chance to shine. Not to mention vegetables, fruit and even the odd legume.

People everywhere are cutting down on sugar in its various forms. In recent years we have become aware that sugar is disguised in many of the products we buy every day. If you look at the ingredients' lists on food packaging, you will see sugars listed in myriad forms – check for raw sugar, brown sugar, sucrose, glucose, fructose, lactose, maltose, dextrose, malt or malt extract. It quickly becomes clear how easy it is to over-consume sugar.

Being mindful of the ingredients we consume and generally eating in moderation is one of the keys to a healthy life. Replacing store-bought, processed products with goodies baked yourself is a step in the right direction.

Now, this is not a health-food book or a diet book; it is a cookbook full of delightful sweet creations that happen to contain less sugar. You'll find recipes in here to suit you if you are wanting to consume less sugar overall, wishing to go fructose-free, or cut sugar from your life completely.

All of the recipes in this book contain less sugar than their traditional equivalent. Many are also gluten free. There are also lots of completely sugar-free options. I have avoided the use of fructose-containing refined cane (or beet) sugar (sucrose) and only used whole and dried fruits. Now, fruit does contain fructose in its natural form, but you get the benefit from the fibre and nutrients as well. By 'refined-sugar free', I mean fructose-free, except for fructose from whole or dried fruit.

Types of sugar
Carbohydrates, along with fat, fibre, protein and water are needed for growth, energy and health; they sustain life and promote health and wellbeing. It is recommended that 50–60 per cent of our total daily energy intake should come from nutrient-dense complex-carbohydrate foods such as wholegrains, fruits and vegetables. Sugars are the simplest carbohydrates, the most basic of which are monosaccharides made up of single molecules and disaccharides (double sugars) consisting of two monosaccharides molecules.

Sucrose
Sucrose is extracted from sugarcane (and beets), and is variously known as table sugar, white sugar, refined sugar, brown sugar, caster (superfine) sugar, icing (confectioners') sugar, raw sugar or sugar, among others. It is also found in fruits and some vegetables. Sucrose is a disaccharide, and the two molecules that make up sucrose are glucose and fructose – 50 per cent each.

Glucose
Glucose is the most plentiful of the simple sugars, found in ripe fruits, some vegetables and honey. It is a monosaccharide. All carbohydrates except for fibre and fructose are eventually converted into glucose by the body. It is our primary fuel and essential to life.

Fructose

Fructose is found in fruits, honey, maple syrup, molasses and agave syrup. It is a monosaccharide and the simplest form of sugar. Fructose and glucose bind together to make sucrose. Fructose comes under particularly close scrutiny and it is the form of sugar we need to be most aware of.

Fructose is metabolised differently in our bodies; unlike glucose that is used by almost every cell, when fructose travels to the liver it is converted into triglycerides (fat) that circulate the body. When we eat more fructose than our bodies can manage (because we are not fully aware of all the 'hidden' sugars we are consuming), our livers become overloaded and we're headed for trouble. The consequences of too much fructose are complex, but put simply, it can contribute to loss of appetite control that may stimulate hunger and lead to overeating. It has been linked to fatty liver disease, cardiovascular problems (increased risk of heart disease and stroke) and type 2 diabetes, to name a few.

Sweeteners used in this book

Natural whole and dried fruit

Whole fruit lends its natural sweetness and moisture to recipes. Homemade puréed apple adds bulk and texture where refined sugar has been removed, especially in cakes. Dried fruit adds little pops of flavour and sweetness.

Rice malt syrup

Rice malt syrup is also known as brown rice syrup. It is made by culturing rice with enzymes to break down the starches, and is then cooked down to create a thick syrup. It has a similar texture to honey and is less sweet on the palate. Unlike honey though, it does not contain fructose. Try to purchase organic rice malt syrup. It is available from health-food stores and supermarkets.

Dextrose

Dextrose is also known as glucose powder or dextrose monohydrate. It is a monosaccharide made up of glucose molecules derived from grains and is less sweet than refined sugar. It does not contain fructose. I have used dextrose in its powdered form in this book. The texture is somewhere between granulated refined sugar and icing (confectioners') sugar. It is available from health-food stores, supermarkets (look in the sports drink aisle), or the 'brewing' aisle in some department stores.

Liquid stevia

Stevia is extracted from the leaves of a plant native to South America. It is super sweet, so you only need between a few drops and up to a teaspoon per recipe. Brands do vary in strength of sweetness and bitterness, so be aware that the particular product you have may take a little bit of trial and error to get the levels that suit you. Stevia is also available in concentrated liquid form (about three times stronger than the liquid I have used), and powdered. I find that the powdered versions vary enormously in strength between brands, so are best avoided for the purposes of this book. Try to purchase organic liquid stevia, as it has less additives. It is available from health-food stores and selected supermarkets.

As you integrate less sugar into your diet, you will find that your sweetness threshold lowers and your palate adjusts. If you do have a sweet tooth, you may sometimes be surprised by the lack of overall sweetness in some of these recipes – if this is the case add a few drops of liquid stevia next time, until you get used to it.

You will find a variety of recipes in this book, suitable for all skill levels and perfect for any number of occasions. There are simple biscuits, cookies and slices that make wonderful teatime and lunchbox treats; fancy cakes to impress your friends and family, suitable for any celebration, or everyday cakes and fruity loaves that should be enjoyed at any time; there are small bakes that are great for feeding a crowd and a collection of sweet endings filled with post-dinner treats. Some recipes do contain a few unexpected savoury ingredients, but don't be put off – I urge you to try them. The natural sweetness and textures given by these ingredients shines through and makes for a satisfying dish that is wholesome and filling.

Please enjoy these incredible bakes with your loved ones, colleagues and friends – they're not just delicious, but better for you too.

Cooking Notes

Baking powder
All baking powder is gluten free.

Butter
All butter is unsalted.

Chocolate and cocoa
There are plenty of chocolaty delights in this book. The chocolate flavour comes from cocoa, chocolate or sometimes a combination of the two. I like to use dark bitter chocolate with a cocoa butter content of 70-85% cocoa solids. It does contain a small amount of sugar. Dutch-processed cocoa has a darker colour and a mellow, deep chocolate taste.

Eggs
All eggs are free-range and extra large (55–60 g/2 oz).

Measurements
All cup and spoon measures are level and based on Australian metric measures: 1 cup = 250 ml (8½ fl oz) and 1 tablespoon = 20 ml (¾ fl oz/4 teaspoons). For best results, weigh your ingredients instead of using cup measures.

Ovens
All oven temperatures are fan-forced. To convert to a conventional oven temperature, increase the temperature by about 20°C (70°F) or check the oven manufacturer's instructions.

Biscuits & Cookies

I was keen on recreating the gingernuts my nanna used to make when I was a kid. They were tooth-breakers, but in a good way. When you remove the white sugar from these guys the texture changes, but I hope Nanna would still recognise them. If it's any indication that they're tasty, my youngest son can't get enough of them.

Ginger biscuits

Makes about 24

300 g (10½ oz/2 cups) plain (all-purpose) flour, plus extra to dust the fork
2 teaspoons ground ginger
½ teaspoon bicarbonate of soda (baking soda)
½ teaspoon salt
125 g (4½ oz) butter, softened
115 g (4 oz/⅓ cup) rice malt syrup
1 teaspoon finely grated fresh ginger
1 egg, lightly beaten
½ teaspoon liquid stevia (optional)

Preheat the oven to 160°C/320°F (fan-forced). Line two baking trays with non-stick baking paper.

Sift the flour, ground ginger, bicarbonate of soda and salt into a large bowl. Set aside.

Beat the butter, rice malt syrup and fresh ginger with an electric mixer until pale and fluffy, scraping down the side of the bowl as necessary. Add the egg gradually, beating well after each addition. Stir in the sifted flour mixture and stevia (if using), until well combined.

Roll tablespoonfuls of the dough into balls and place on the prepared trays about 4 cm (1½ in) apart. Flatten the balls with a fork dusted with flour to about 1.5 cm (½ in) thick. Bake for 15–18 minutes or until starting to colour around the edges. Remove from the oven and leave to cool on the trays for 5 minutes. Transfer to a wire rack to cool completely.

These biscuits will keep for up to a week in an airtight container.

There's something about the texture of polenta that I find addictive. I like cutting these shortbreads into flower shapes, but you can use any cutters you have available. If the dough becomes too warm and difficult to handle, wrap it in plastic wrap and pop it in the refrigerator for 10 minutes to firm up.

Crunchy lemon & polenta shortbread flowers

Makes about 20

125 g (4½ oz) butter, softened
40 g (1½ oz/¼ cup) dextrose
1½ teaspoons finely grated lemon zest
110 g (4 oz/¾ cup) plain (all-purpose) flour
75 g (2¾ oz/½ cup) brown rice flour
40 g (1½ oz/¼ cup) fine polenta (cornmeal), plus extra to sprinkle

Preheat the oven to 160°C/320°F (fan-forced). Line two baking trays with non-stick baking paper.

Beat the butter, dextrose and lemon zest with an electric mixer until pale and fluffy, scraping down the side of the bowl as necessary.

Combine the two flours and the polenta in a separate bowl, then gradually add to the butter mixture until combined. Turn the dough out onto a clean work surface and knead gently until smooth.

Roll the dough between two sheets of non-stick baking paper to a thickness of about 5 mm (¼ in). Cut out shapes with your cookie cutter of choice, re-rolling the dough as necessary.

Carefully transfer the shapes to the prepared trays using a small spatula and place about 3 cm (1¼ in) apart. Sprinkle with a little extra polenta and bake for 8–10 minutes or until cooked through and just starting to colour. Remove from the oven and leave to cool on the trays for 10 minutes. Transfer to a wire rack to cool completely.

These biscuits will keep for up to a week in an airtight container.

A sweet biscuit with cracked peppercorns may sound a bit unusual, but rest assured these biscuits have an intriguing and delicious flavour with a slight kick. If you don't have a mortar and pestle, coarsely grind the peppercorns in a pepper grinder. Fresh strawberries are a great accompaniment.

Cracked pepper biscuits

Makes about 25

125 g (4½ oz) butter, softened
2 tablespoons rice malt syrup
1 teaspoon mixed peppercorns
110 g (4 oz/¾ cup) plain (all-purpose) spelt flour
50 g (1¾ oz/⅓ cup) cornflour (cornstarch)
dextrose to sprinkle (optional)

Preheat the oven to 160°C/320°F (fan-forced). Line two baking trays with non-stick baking paper.

Beat the butter and rice malt syrup with an electric mixer until well combined, scraping down the side of the bowl as necessary.

Crush the peppercorns in a mortar and pestle. Sift the flours into the butter mixture, add the peppercorns and mix on low speed until combined. Pop the mixture in the refrigerator for 10 minutes or so, if it is too soft to roll.

Roll 2 teaspoonfuls of the dough into balls and place on the prepared trays about 3 cm (1¼ in) apart. Flatten slightly with your fingertips and bake for 8–10 minutes, or until the biscuits are just starting to colour around the edges. Remove from the oven and sprinkle with the dextrose, if desired, while still hot. Leave to cool on the trays.

These biscuits will keep for up to a week in an airtight container.

Cacao nibs give a chocolaty punch without the added sugar. I especially love their crunchy texture and slight bitterness. You can add chunks of 70–85% dark chocolate if you prefer.

Cacao nib hazelnut cookies

Makes about 25
Gluten free

100 g (3½ oz) hazelnuts
125 g (4½ oz) butter, softened
115 g (4 oz/⅓ cup) rice malt syrup
2 teaspoons natural vanilla extract
1 egg, beaten
150 g (5½ oz/1 cup) gluten-free plain (all-purpose) flour
75 g (2¾ oz/¾ cup) hazelnut meal
1 teaspoon baking powder
½ teaspoon salt
55 g (2 oz/⅓ cup) cacao nibs

Preheat the oven to 160°C/320°F (fan-forced). Line two baking trays with non-stick baking paper.

Spread the hazelnuts over one of the trays and toast for 5–8 minutes or until fragrant and the skins have loosened. Let the nuts cool slightly then rub them in a clean dish towel to remove the skins. Discard the skins and roughly chop the nuts. Retain the sheet of baking paper for baking the cookies.

Beat the butter, rice malt syrup and vanilla extract with an electric mixer until pale and fluffy, scraping down the side of the bowl as necessary.

Add the egg gradually, beating well between each addition. Sift the flour, hazelnut meal, baking powder and salt into the mixture. Add the chopped hazelnuts and cacao nibs and stir until well combined.

Drop tablespoonfuls of the mixture onto the prepared trays about 4 cm (1½ in) apart. Flatten slightly with a fingertip dipped in water and bake for 18–20 minutes or until just starting to colour around the edges. Remove from the oven and leave to cool on the trays for 5 minutes. Transfer to a wire rack to cool completely.

These cookies will keep for up to a week in an airtight container.

This super crunchy almond bread makes a great accompaniment to a refreshing fruit salad at the end of a meal. I love the natural sweetness of almonds, but if you feel like you need a touch more, add ½ teaspoon liquid stevia with the almonds. Almond bread requires two rounds of cooking, so turn off your oven while the bread cools after the first bake.

Almond bread

Makes about 50

4 egg whites
¼ teaspoon cream of tartar
80 g (2¾ oz/½ cup) dextrose
200 g (7 oz/1¼ cups) whole natural almonds
150 g (5½ oz/1 cup) plain (all-purpose) flour
pinch of salt

Preheat the oven to 160°C/320°F (fan-forced). Grease a small loaf (bar) tin (11.5 cm x 21.5 cm/4½ in x 8½ in; 1.25 litre/42 fl oz capacity) and line the base and two long sides with a piece of non-stick baking paper, extending the paper about 4 cm (1½ in) above the sides of the tin to assist with the removal of the cooked bread.

Beat the egg whites and cream of tartar with an electric mixer until soft peaks form. Gradually add the dextrose and beat until stiff peaks form. Do not over-beat.

Gently fold in the almonds, flour and salt. Do not over-mix – try to retain as much air in the egg whites as you can.

Spread into the prepared tin and bake for 35–40 minutes or until lightly browned and firm to touch. Remove from the oven and transfer to a wire rack to cool. Turn off the oven.

When you are ready for the second bake, preheat the oven to 110°C/230°F (fan-forced) and line two baking trays with non-stick baking paper.

Slice the cool bread as thinly as you can – a long serrated knife is best. Place the slices on the prepared baking trays and bake for a further 30–35 minutes, turning the slices over after 20 minutes, until dried out. Remove from the oven and transfer to a wire rack to cool completely.

This almond bread will keep for up to a week in an airtight container.

These cookies are a dream come true for fans of peanut butter! Make sure you buy peanut butter made from 100 per cent peanuts.

Peanut butter cookies

Makes about 24
Gluten free

280 g (10 oz/1 cup) crunchy natural peanut butter
115 g (4 oz/⅓ cup) rice malt syrup
1 teaspoon natural vanilla extract
50 g (1¾ oz/⅓ cup) cornflour (cornstarch)
1 teaspoon baking powder
100 g (3½ oz) dark chocolate (70–85% cocoa solids), chopped into chunks
70 g (2½ oz/½ cup) roasted salted peanuts

Preheat the oven to 160°C/320°F (fan-forced). Line two baking trays with non-stick baking paper.

Combine the peanut butter, rice malt syrup and vanilla extract in a large bowl. Add the cornflour and baking powder and mix well. Stir in the chocolate and peanuts until well combined. Using your hands may make this job easier.

Roll tablespoonfuls of the dough into balls and place on the prepared trays about 4 cm (1½ in) apart. Flatten the balls lightly with your fingertips to about 1.5 cm (½ in) thick. Poke in any peanuts or bits of chocolate left behind in the bowl. Bake for 8–10 minutes or until just starting to colour around the edges. Remove from the oven and leave to cool on the trays for 10 minutes. Transfer to a wire rack to cool completely.

These cookies will keep for up to a week in an airtight container.

Left to right
Almond bread;
Peanut butter cookies

The mellow and warm comforting flavour of brown butter works beautifully with pecans in this easy melt 'n' mix shortbread.

Brown butter pecan shortbread fingers

Makes 24

250 g (9 oz) butter, chopped
335 g (12 oz/2¼ cups) plain (all-purpose) flour
80 g (2¾ oz/½ cup) dextrose
50 g (1¾ oz/⅓ cup) cornflour (cornstarch)
90 g (3 oz/¾ cup) coarsely chopped pecans
1 teaspoon vanilla bean paste

Preheat the oven to 160°C/320°F (fan-forced). Grease an 18 cm x 28 cm (7 in x 11 in) slice tin and line the base and two long sides with a piece of non-stick baking paper, extending the paper about 4 cm (1½ in) above the sides of the tin to assist with the removal of the cooked shortbread.

Heat the butter in a small saucepan over low heat until the butter melts and the milk solids (the little specks that separate from the liquid portion of the butter) become a nut-brown colour and give off a delicious nutty aroma. Swirl the pan so you can see the colour of the solids through the foam. Remove from the heat and immediately dunk the base of the pan in a sink of cold water to stop the cooking process.

Mix the flour, dextrose and cornflour in a bowl until combined. Add the melted butter, pecans and vanilla bean paste and mix well.

Press the mixture into the prepared tin, smooth over with a spatula and bake for 25–30 minutes or until lightly browned and firm to touch. Remove from the oven and put on a wire rack to cool in the tin. Cut into slices while still warm and still in the tin.

This shortbread will keep for up to a week in an airtight container.

These biscuits are perfect for when you don't quite have the appetite for a slice of cake, but you still fancy a treat. They are slightly chewy around the edges and more cake-like and soft in the centre. The mixture is great to freeze in portions, and then bake on demand.

Carrot cake biscuits

Makes about 20
Gluten free

125 g (4½ oz) butter, softened
85 g (3 oz/¼ cup) rice malt syrup
1 egg, lightly beaten
75 g (2¾ oz/½ cup) coconut flour
1 teaspoon baking powder
1 teaspoon mixed spice
½ teaspoon ground ginger
100 g (3½ oz) dried dates, chopped
1 small carrot (about 70 g/2½ oz), grated

Beat the butter and rice malt syrup with an electric mixer until pale and fluffy, scraping down the side of the bowl as necessary.

Add the egg gradually, beating well between each addition. Sift the flour, baking powder, mixed spice and ginger into the butter mixture. Add the dates and carrot and stir until well combined. Cover and chill in the refrigerator for about 1 hour or until firm enough to roll.

Preheat the oven to 170°C/340°F (fan-forced). Line two baking trays with non-stick baking paper.

Roll tablespoonfuls of the dough into balls and place on the prepared trays about 4 cm (1½ in) apart. Flatten to about 1 cm (½ in) thick and bake for 15–20 minutes or until just starting to colour around the edges. Remove from the oven and cool on the trays.

These biscuits will keep for 3–4 days in an airtight container.

Melting moments are a nostalgic favourite of mine. They've been given a whole new lease of life here with delicious passionfruit cashew cream. Try the cashew cream as an icing for cupcakes, a cake filling or even on your toasted sourdough for breakfast.

Passionfruit cashew cream melting moments

Makes about 12

125 g (4½ oz) butter, softened
2 tablespoons rice malt syrup
2 teaspoons vanilla bean paste
110 g (4 oz/¾ cup) plain (all-purpose) spelt flour
50 g (1¾ oz/⅓ cup) cornflour (cornstarch), plus extra for dusting the fork

Passionfruit cashew cream
75 g (2¾ oz/½ cup) raw cashews
2–3 passionfruit
2 teaspoons rice malt syrup

For the passionfruit cashew cream, soak the cashews in cold water for 1 hour. Strain the passionfruit, keeping both the juice and the seeds. You will need about 1 tablespoon of passionfruit juice. Drain the cashews, rinse well and drain again. Put the cashews in a blender with the passionfruit juice and blend until smooth. Add a little more passionfruit juice or water to balance the flavour (it should have a tangy kick) and to get a thick, spreadable consistency. Stir in the passionfruit seeds. Transfer to a bowl and pop in the refrigerator, covered, until required.

Meanwhile, preheat the oven to 160°C/320°F (fan-forced). Line two baking trays with non-stick baking paper.

Beat the butter, rice malt syrup and vanilla bean paste with an electric mixer until well combined, scraping down the side of the bowl as necessary.

Sift the flours into the butter mixture and mix on low speed until combined.

Roll 2 teaspoonfuls of the dough into balls and place on the prepared trays about 3 cm (1¼ in) apart. If you find the mixture slightly too sticky to roll, particularly if the weather is hot, chill in the refrigerator for 15 minutes or so to firm up. With a fork dipped in extra cornflour, flatten the balls lightly to about 1 cm (½ in) thick. Bake for 10–12 minutes or until just starting to colour around the edges. Remove from the oven and leave to cool on the trays.

Before serving, spread a little of the passionfruit cashew cream on half of the biscuits. Place the remaining biscuits on top of the cream and sandwich the biscuits together.

The unfilled biscuits will keep for up to a week in an airtight container. The passionfruit cashew cream will keep in a sealed container in the refrigerator for up to 2 days.

Roasting the cocoa adds extra depth to these rich and dark chocolate cookies.

Roasted cocoa crackle cookies

Makes about 20

30 g (1 oz/⅓ cup) cocoa powder (unsweetened)
110 g (4 oz/¾ cup) plain (all-purpose) flour, plus extra for dusting the fork
½ teaspoon bicarbonate of soda (baking soda)
200 g (7 oz) dark chocolate (70–85% cocoa solids), chopped
60 g (2 oz) butter
115 g (4 oz/⅓ cup) rice malt syrup
1 egg
2 teaspoons natural vanilla extract
½ teaspoon liquid stevia

Preheat the oven to 160°C/320°F (fan-forced). Line two baking trays with non-stick baking paper.

Spread the cocoa in a thin layer over one of the prepared trays. Bake for 20–25 minutes until the cocoa is dark brown and fragrant, stirring every 5 minutes. Transfer to a small bowl and set aside to cool. Retain the sheet of baking paper for baking the cookies.

Sift the flour, bicarbonate of soda and cooled cocoa into a large bowl. Set aside.

Melt 100 g (3½ oz) of the chocolate and all of the butter together in a small heavy-based saucepan over low heat. Remove from the heat and pour into a large bowl. Whisk in the rice malt syrup, egg, vanilla extract and stevia, then stir in the sifted flour mixture until combined. Cover and put in the refrigerator for about 1 hour or until the mixture is firm enough to roll.

Roll tablespoonfuls of the dough into balls and place on the prepared trays about 4 cm (1½ in) apart. With a fork dipped in extra flour, flatten the balls lightly to about 1.5 cm (½ in) thick. Bake for 13–15 minutes, or until cooked through. Remove from the oven and leave to cool on the trays for 10 minutes. Transfer to a wire rack to cool completely.

Melt the remaining chocolate in a small heatproof bowl over a saucepan of simmering water. Drizzle the chocolate over the cooled cookies. Allow the chocolate to set before serving.

These cookies will keep for up to a week in an airtight container.

You can try endless flavour variations in these moreish cookies. Experiment with dried blueberries, sour cherries, chopped dried apricots or even a handful of nuts.

Chewy oat cookies

Makes about 20

150 g (5½ oz/1 cup) plain (all-purpose) flour
100 g (3½ oz/1 cup) rolled (porridge) oats
40 g (1½ oz/½ cup) shredded coconut
70 g (2½ oz/½ cup) dried unsweetened cranberries
125 g (4½ oz) butter, chopped
115 g (4 oz/⅓ cup) rice malt syrup
½ teaspoon bicarbonate of soda (baking soda)

Preheat the oven to 160°C/320°F (fan-forced). Line two baking trays with non-stick baking paper.

Combine the flour, rolled oats, coconut and dried cranberries in a large bowl.

Stir the butter and rice malt syrup in a small saucepan over low heat until melted and combined. Mix in the bicarbonate of soda then, when frothy, add to the oat mixture and stir until well combined.

Roll tablespoonfuls of the dough into balls and place on the prepared trays about 4 cm (1½ in) apart. Press down lightly with your fingertips to flatten the balls to about 1.5 cm (½ in) thick. Bake for 12–15 minutes or until the edges start to colour slightly. Remove from the oven and leave to cool on the trays for 10 minutes. Transfer to a wire rack to cool completely.

These biscuits will keep for up to a week in an airtight container.

You can enjoy these chocolate shortbread biscuits by themselves, or even drizzled with dark chocolate; however, filling them with banana cashew cream is even better! They also work perfectly filled with the tangy Passionfruit cashew cream on page 28; just make a double batch of the cream/filling.

Chocolate shortbread sandwich biscuits with banana cashew cream

Makes about 14

260 g (9 oz/1¾ cups) plain (all-purpose) flour
35 g (1¼ oz/⅓ cup) Dutch-processed cocoa powder
200 g (7 oz) butter, softened
80 g (2¾ oz/½ cup) dextrose
¼ teaspoon liquid stevia

Banana cashew cream
150 g (5½ oz/1 cup) raw cashews
½ banana (about 60 g/2 oz), mashed
about 1 tablespoon freshly squeezed lemon juice

For the banana cashew cream, soak the cashews in cold water for 1 hour. Drain the cashews, rinse well and drain again. Put the cashews in a blender with the banana and most of the lemon juice and blend until smooth. Add a little more lemon juice or water to balance the flavour (it should have a slight tangy kick) and to get a thick, spreadable consistency. Transfer to a bowl and pop it in the refrigerator, covered, until required.

Meanwhile, preheat the oven to 140°C/275°F (fan-forced). Line two baking trays with non-stick baking paper.

Sift the flour and cocoa powder into a large bowl. Set aside.

Beat the butter, dextrose and stevia with an electric mixer until light and creamy, scraping down the side of the bowl as necessary. Add the sifted flour and cocoa in two batches and mix on low speed until just combined and the mixture has a crumble-like appearance. Transfer to a clean work surface and knead lightly to bring the dough together.

Divide the dough in half and roll between two sheets of non-stick baking paper to 5 mm (¼ in) thick. Cut into rounds using a 6.5 cm (2½ in) cookie cutter, re-rolling the dough as necessary. You should get about 28 rounds. Put the cookies on the prepared trays as you go, about 2 cm (¾ in) apart. If you find the mixture becomes too soft to roll, particularly if the weather is hot, chill the mixture for 15 minutes or so to firm up and then continue.

Bake for 20–25 minutes or until cooked through. Remove from the oven and leave to cool on the trays.

Before serving, spread a little of the banana cashew cream on half of the biscuits. Place the remaining biscuits on top of the cream and sandwich the biscuits together.

The unfilled biscuits will keep for up to a week in an airtight container. The banana cashew cream will keep in a sealed container in the refrigerator for up to 2 days.

Left to right
Chewy oat cookies;
Chocolate shortbread
sandwich biscuits

These biscotti are perfect for dipping into your coffee. They're really crunchy with a slightly savoury edge due to the rosemary. Biscotti require two rounds of baking, so turn off your oven while the biscuit logs cool after the first bake.

Rosemary, hazelnut & orange biscotti

Makes about 40

2 eggs, lightly beaten
115 g (4 oz/⅓ cup) rice malt syrup
1 teaspoon finely grated orange zest
2 teaspoons finely chopped fresh rosemary
½ teaspoon liquid stevia
300 g (10½ oz/2 cups) plain (all-purpose) flour
¼ teaspoon baking powder
100 g (3½ oz) hazelnuts
50 g (1¾ oz/⅓ cup) pine nuts

Preheat the oven to 160°C/320°F (fan-forced). Line two baking trays with non-stick baking paper.

Whisk the egg, rice malt syrup, orange zest and rosemary together in a large bowl. Sift the flour and baking powder into the bowl, then add the hazelnuts and pine nuts, and mix to form a smooth firm dough.

Divide the dough in half and roll each half into a slightly flattened log, about 20 cm (8 in) long. Place the logs of dough on one of the prepared trays and bake for 30 minutes or until lightly browned and firm to touch. Remove from the oven and leave to cool on the tray. Turn off the oven.

When the biscuit logs are cool, preheat the oven to 160°C/320°F (fan-forced). On a chopping board, cut the logs diagonally into 5 mm (¼ in) thick slices with a serrated knife. Put the slices in a single layer on the prepared trays and bake for a further 20–25 minutes, turning the slices over after 10 minutes, until crisp. Remove from the oven and transfer to a wire rack to cool completely.

These biscotti will keep for up to two weeks in an airtight container.

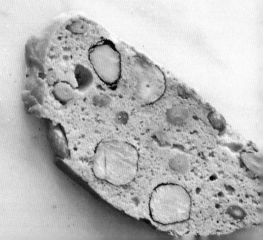

I can't get enough of tahini. These delicious little morsels are reminiscent of halva, but without the sugar. If you want them to be more than a mouthful, by all means double the size.

Tahini shortbread buttons

Makes about 40
Gluten free

100 g (3½ oz) butter, softened
80 g (2¾ oz/½ cup) dextrose
1 teaspoon vanilla bean paste
90 g (3 oz/¼ cup) tahini
150 g (5½ oz/1 cup) gluten-free plain (all-purpose) flour
60 g (2 oz/½ cup) almond meal
1½ tablespoons white sesame seeds
1½ tablespoons roasted black sesame seeds

Preheat the oven to 160°C/320°F (fan-forced). Line three baking trays with non-stick baking paper.

Beat the butter, dextrose and vanilla bean paste with an electric mixer until pale and fluffy, scraping down the side of the bowl as necessary. Add the tahini and beat until well combined. Mix in the flour and almond meal until well combined. Knead lightly in the bowl with your hand to bring the dough together, if necessary.

Combine the sesame seeds in a small bowl.

Roll 2 teaspoonfuls of the dough into balls and flatten with your fingertips to about 1 cm (½ in) thick. Roll the edges of the dough in the combined sesame seeds and place on the prepared trays about 3 cm (1¼ in) apart. Bake for 18–20 minutes or until just starting to colour around the edges. Remove from the oven and leave to cool on the trays for 10 minutes. Transfer to wire racks to cool completely.

These biscuits will keep for up to a week in an airtight container.

Toasting and grinding the whole natural almonds gives these cookies an added dimension. I like them with no added sweetness whatsoever, but by all means add ¼ teaspoon liquid stevia with the vanilla extract, if you like.

Toasted almond, coconut & chia cookies

Makes about 20
Gluten free

200 g (7 oz/1¼ cups) whole natural almonds
40 g (1½ oz/½ cup) shredded coconut
1 tablespoon chia seeds
1 teaspoon baking powder
¼ teaspoon salt
1 egg, lightly beaten
1 tablespoon melted virgin coconut oil
1 teaspoon natural vanilla extract
¼ teaspoon liquid stevia (optional)

Preheat the oven to 160°C/320°F (fan-forced). Line two baking trays with non-stick baking paper.

Put the almonds on one of the trays and toast for 8–10 minutes or until fragrant. Transfer to a small bowl and set aside to cool. Retain the sheet of baking paper for baking the cookies.

Pulse the cooled almonds in a food processor until finely ground, then transfer to a bowl. Add the coconut, chia seeds, baking powder and salt and mix until combined. Add the egg, coconut oil, vanilla extract and stevia, if using, and mix until well combined.

Drop tablespoonfuls of the dough onto the prepared trays about 3 cm (1¼ in) apart. Shape the dough into rounds about 1 cm (½ in) thick.

Bake for 8–10 minutes or until just starting to colour around the edges. Remove from the oven and leave to cool on the trays.

These biscuits will keep for up to a week in an airtight container.

Small Bakes

These brownies are dense, but not heavy. They're quite rich, so you won't need much to feel satisfied – the perfect match for a cup of coffee.

Brownies with coconut–date swirl

Serves 16
Gluten free

280 g (10 oz/2 cups) seedless dried dates, roughly chopped
1 teaspoon bicarbonate of soda (baking soda)
250 ml (8½ fl oz/1 cup) boiling water
2 eggs
80 ml (2½ fl oz/⅓ cup) macadamia oil
100 g (3½ oz/⅔ cup) coconut flour
3 teaspoons baking powder
cream or coconut cream, to serve (optional)

Coconut–date swirl
70 g (2½ oz/½ cup) seedless dried dates, roughly chopped
125 ml (4 fl oz/½ cup) coconut milk

Preheat the oven to 160°C/320°F (fan-forced). Grease an 18 cm (7 in) square shallow cake tin and line the base and two opposite sides with a piece of non-stick baking paper, extending the paper about 4 cm (1½ in) above the sides of the tin to assist with the removal of the cooked brownie.

Put the dates in a small heatproof bowl and stir in the bicarbonate of soda and boiling water. Set aside for 10 minutes to cool. Mash well with a fork.

Meanwhile, for the coconut–date swirl, put the dates and coconut milk in a small saucepan. Bring to the boil over low heat, stirring often, then remove from the heat and set aside to cool for 10 minutes. Mash well with a fork.

Whisk the eggs and the oil together in a bowl, then whisk in the mashed dates. Sift in the coconut flour and baking powder and stir to combine.

Spread the mixture into the prepared tin and dollop spoonfuls of the coconut–date swirl mixture over the top. Swirl lightly with the tip of a small knife. Bake for 25–30 minutes or until just firm to the touch and a skewer inserted into the centre comes out almost clean. Remove from the oven and leave to cool for 10 minutes before gently lifting onto a wire rack to cool completely. Cut into squares and serve with cream or coconut cream, if desired.

These brownies will keep for up to 1 week in an airtight container in the refrigerator.

The cannellini (lima) beans are a surprising ingredient that lends a great texture to these blondies, which are very tender and moist.

Banana chai blondies

Serves 16
Gluten free

400 g (14 oz) tin cannellini (lima) beans, rinsed and drained
1 ripe banana, peeled
80 g (2¾ oz) butter, softened
3 eggs
50 g (1¾ oz/½ cup) desiccated (dried shredded) coconut
1 teaspoon baking powder
1 teaspoon ground star anise
½ teaspoon ground cinnamon
½ teaspoon ground ginger
½ teaspoon liquid stevia
1 tablespoon cacao nibs

Preheat the oven to 160°C/320°F (fan-forced). Grease a 19 cm (7½ in) square shallow cake tin and line the base and two opposite sides with a piece of non-stick baking paper, extending the paper about 4 cm (1½ in) above the sides of the tin to assist with the removal of the cooked blondie.

Whiz the beans, banana and butter in a food processor until smooth and creamy. Add the eggs, coconut, baking powder, spices and stevia. Process until combined. The mixture may look curdled, but don't worry, it will be fine.

Pour the mixture into the prepared tin, sprinkle with cacao nibs and bake for 20–25 minutes or until just firm to the touch and a skewer inserted into the centre comes out clean. Remove from the oven and cool for 10 minutes before gently lifting onto a wire rack to cool completely. Cut into pieces to serve.

These blondies will keep for up to a week in an airtight container in the refrigerator.

This tender and slightly crumbly slice is delicious with a hot cup of tea or coffee. Make this slice gluten-free by replacing the plain (all-purpose) flour with gluten-free plain flour plus 1 teaspoon of xanthan gum.

Fig, prune & cranberry crumble slice

Makes 16

150 g (5½ oz/¾ cup) whole dried figs, chopped
110 g (4 oz/⅔ cup) seeded prunes, roughly chopped
45 g (1½ oz/⅓ cup) dried unsweetened cranberries
125 ml (4 fl oz/½ cup) boiling water
200 g (7 oz) butter, softened
2 tablespoons rice malt syrup
225 g (8 oz/1½ cups) plain (all-purpose) flour
½ teaspoon baking powder
150 g (5½ oz/1½ cups) rolled (porridge) oats
cocoa powder (unsweetened), to dust (optional)

Put the fruit in a small heatproof bowl. Add the boiling water and set aside to plump up for 30 minutes or until cool, stirring occasionally. Mash the fruit roughly together. The mixture will be quite lumpy.

Preheat the oven to 160°C/320°F (fan-forced). Grease a 19 cm (7½ in) square shallow cake tin and line the base and two opposite sides with a piece of non-stick baking paper, extending the paper about 4 cm (1½ in) above the sides of the tin to assist with the removal of the cooked slice.

Meanwhile, beat the butter and rice malt syrup together with an electric mixer until pale and fluffy, scraping down the sides of the bowl as necessary. Sift together the flour and baking powder. Add to the butter mixture along with the oats and use a wooden spoon to mix until combined. Use your hands to make this job easier if you like.

Spoon half of the crumble mixture into the prepared tin and use the back of a spoon to press evenly over the base. Spread with the fruit mixture, and then sprinkle the remaining crumble mixture over the top, keeping it in little clumps.

Bake for 30–35 minutes or until the top seems firm to touch (this slice will not brown much as it is cooking). Remove from the oven and, leaving the slice in the tin, place on a wire rack to cool completely.

Dust with cocoa, if you like, and cut into squares before serving.

This slice will keep for 3–4 days in an airtight container.

This is similar to the classic coconut jam slice, except this one is gluten free and made with chia jam. It is slightly softer, but just as moreish. Try it with a drizzle of cream or a dollop of thick, creamy yoghurt for the perfect match.

Coconut raspberry jam slice

Makes 16
Gluten free

150 g (5½ oz/½ cup) Apple purée (page 162)
100 g (3½ oz/⅔ cup) coconut flour
60 g (2 oz/½ cup) almond meal
60 ml (2 fl oz/¼ cup) melted virgin coconut oil
2 tablespoons rice malt syrup
2 teaspoons baking powder
2 teaspoons natural vanilla extract
2 eggs
90 g (3 oz/1 cup) desiccated (dried shredded) coconut
80 g (2¾ oz/1 cup) shredded coconut
420 g (15 oz/1½ cups) Raspberry chia jam (page 163)

Preheat the oven to 160°C/320°F (fan-forced). Grease an 18 cm x 26 cm (7 in x 10¼ in) slice tin and line the base and two opposite sides with a piece of non-stick baking paper, extending the paper about 4 cm (1½ in) above the sides of the tin to assist with the removal of the cooked slice.

Combine the apple purée, flour, almond meal, oil, rice malt syrup, baking powder and vanilla in a bowl. Mix until a dough forms. Put the mixture into the prepared tin and use the back of a spoon to press evenly over the base. Bake for 10–15 minutes or until firm to touch and golden around the edges. Remove from the oven and set aside to cool slightly.

Whisk the eggs until frothy and stir in the desiccated and shredded coconut. Spread the slightly cooled base with the jam and sprinkle the coconut mixture over the top. Bake for a further 15–20 minutes or until the coconut mixture is set and golden brown.

Remove from the oven and, leaving the slice in the tin, place on a wire rack to cool completely.

This slice will keep for 3–4 days in an airtight container in the refrigerator.

Beetroot (beets) and chocolate are great partners. These brownies have a
real decadence about them, with a great fudgy texture grounded by the earthy
flavour of the beetroot. You can add a handful of roughly chopped pecans
or macadamias for crunch if you like. They're lovely served with a dollop
of thick creamy yoghurt.

Beetroot chocolate brownies

Makes 16

80 ml (2½ fl oz/⅓ cup) macadamia oil
3 eggs
1 teaspoon natural vanilla extract
½ teaspoon liquid stevia
100 g (3½ oz) dark chocolate (70–85% cocoa solids), melted
2 beetroot (beets) (about 350 g/12½ oz), peeled and finely grated
1 large apple (about 200 g/7 oz), grated with skin on
110 g (4 oz/¾ cup) plain (all-purpose) spelt flour
2 tablespoons raw cacao powder, plus extra to dust
1 teaspoon baking powder

Preheat the oven to 160°C/320°F (fan-forced). Grease a 20 cm x 30 cm (8 in x 12 in) slice tin and line the
base and two long sides with a piece of non-stick baking paper, extending the paper about 4 cm (1½ in)
over the sides of the tin to assist with the removal of the cooked brownie.

Whisk the oil, eggs, vanilla extract and stevia together in a bowl until well combined. Add the melted
chocolate and the beetroot and apple and stir to combine. Sift the flour, cacao and baking powder over
the mixture and fold until combined.

Spread the mixture into the prepared tin and bake for 15–20 minutes or until just firm to the touch.
Remove from the oven and cool for 10 minutes before gently lifting onto a wire rack to cool. Cut into
pieces and serve dusted with extra cacao if you like.

These brownies will keep for up to a week in an airtight container in the refrigerator.

This is my guilt-free version of a jam donut, disguised as a muffin. These are best straight from the oven, but reheat quite well in the microwave.

Jam duffins

Makes 9

150 g (5½ oz/1 cup) plain (all-purpose) flour
100 g (3½ oz/⅔ cup) wholemeal (whole-wheat) flour
2 teaspoons baking powder
½ teaspoon ground cinnamon
1 large apple (about 200 g/7 oz), grated with the skin on
180 ml (6 fl oz/¾ cup) buttermilk
2 eggs
50 g (1¾ oz) butter, melted
2 teaspoons natural vanilla extract
½ teaspoon liquid stevia (optional)
2½ tablespoons Raspberry chia jam (page 163)

Cinnamon powder
1 tablespoon dextrose
2 teaspoons ground cinnamon

Preheat the oven to 160°C/320°F (fan-forced). Lightly grease a 9-hole 80 ml (2½ fl oz/⅓ cup capacity) muffin tin.

Sift the flours, baking powder and cinnamon into a bowl, returning the husks from the wholemeal flour to the sifted mixture, then stir in the apple.

Whisk the buttermilk, eggs, butter, vanilla extract and stevia (if using) together in a separate bowl or jug. Pour into the flour mixture and stir with a large spoon until just combined. Do not over-mix.

Spoon most of the batter (reserving about 1 tablespoon for adding to the top of the duffins later) into the prepared tray. Make a small hole in the top of each duffin with the handle-end of a teaspoon and add about 1 teaspoon of jam to each hole. Cover jam gently with the reserved batter.

Bake for 15–20 minutes or until duffins spring back when lightly pressed. Remove from the oven and cool for 2 minutes in the tin before carefully removing. Roll duffins gently in the combined cinnamon powder ingredients and serve immediately.

These duffins are best served warm from the oven, however they will keep for 2–3 days in an airtight container in the refrigerator. Reheat before serving.

Left to right
**Beetroot chocolate
brownies; Jam duffins**

Super crunchy and packed with protein from seeds and grains, these bars are a tasty energy source after a hard workout or a long walk, or for a relatively healthy snack. It might seem a bit weird to include cumin in a non-savoury recipe, but it gives a slightly unusual edge to these bars.

Superfood bars

Makes 20
Wheat free

40 g (1½ oz/¼ cup) sesame seeds
100 g (3½ oz/½ cup) raw unhulled buckwheat
150 g (5½ oz/1½ cups) rolled (porridge) oats
65 g (2¼ oz/¾ cup) quinoa flakes
45 g (1½ oz/⅓ cup) roughly chopped cashews
45 g (1½ oz/¼ cup) pepitas (pumpkin seeds)
40 g (1½ oz/½ cup) shredded coconut
2 tablespoons chia seeds
2 tablespoons sunflower seed kernels
3 teaspoons ground cinnamon
2 teaspoons ground ginger
1 teaspoon ground cumin
1 teaspoon cumin seeds
2 tablespoons melted virgin coconut oil
2 tablespoons tahini
170 g (6 oz/½ cup) rice malt syrup

Preheat the oven to 140°C/275°F (fan-forced). Grease a 20 x 30 cm (8 in x 12 in) slice tin and line the base and two long sides with a piece of non-stick baking paper, extending the paper about 4 cm (1½ in) above the sides of the tin to assist with the removal of the cooked slice.

Reserving 1 tablespoon of the sesame seeds for sprinkling over the top, combine the remaining sesame seeds and all of the remaining dry ingredients in a large bowl. Add the coconut oil and tahini and mix well until all the ingredients are coated. Drizzle the rice malt syrup over and mix until well combined. If you use your hands this job will be easier.

Using the back of a large spoon, press the mixture firmly and evenly into the prepared tin. Sprinkle with the reserved sesame seeds and press them into the surface.

Bake for 25–30 minutes or until the top is firm to touch and lightly browned. Leave the slice in the tin and, while still warm, cut into 20 bars. Place the tin on a wire rack to cool completely.

These bars will keep for up to a week in an airtight container.

These are more like lovely little almond cakes than donuts, but they work really well in the ring shape. If rosewater is not your thing, leave it out and add a little more vanilla extract. Rosewater can vary in strength, so add it to taste, with some caution.

Almond, rosewater & chocolate donut cakes

Makes 12
Gluten free

melted butter, for greasing
4 eggs
115 g (4 oz/⅓ cup) rice malt syrup
240 g (8½ oz/2 cups) almond meal
2 teaspoons baking powder
1 teaspoon natural vanilla extract
about 1 teaspoon rosewater
edible dried rose petals and slivered pistachios, to decorate

Chocolate glaze
100 g (3½ oz) dark chocolate (70–85% cocoa solids), chopped
125 ml (4 fl oz/½ cup) thickened (double/heavy) cream

Preheat the oven to 160°C/320°F (fan-forced). Generously grease two 6-hole 80 ml (2½ fl oz/⅓ cup) capacity donut tins with the melted butter. (If you don't have two, don't worry, they will be fine cooked in two batches.)

Whisk the eggs and rice malt syrup together until the syrup dissolves. Stir in the almond meal, baking powder, vanilla extract and rosewater to taste.

Put the batter in a piping bag fitted with a 1.5 cm (½ in) plain nozzle (or use a large sealable plastic bag with the corner snipped off) and pipe the mixture into the prepared donut holes (alternatively, you can spoon the batter in). Fill each hole about two-thirds full.

Bake for 10–12 minutes or until well-risen and just firm to touch. Remove from the oven and set aside to cool in the tin for 15 minutes. Carefully loosen the donuts and turn onto a wire rack to cool completely.

For the chocolate glaze, put the chocolate in a small heatproof bowl. Heat the cream in a small saucepan over medium heat and bring just to the boil. Pour over the chocolate and stir until melted and combined. Set aside to cool and thicken slightly, if necessary.

Dip the cooled donuts into the glaze and sprinkle with rose petals and slivered pistachios.

These donut cakes will keep for 2–3 days in an airtight container.

These cupcakes are super moist and chocolaty. If you feel like adding a pink tinge to the topping, squeeze a little bit of juice from the grated beetroot (beet) and stir it into the topping mixture. Soak and cook your own cannellini (lima) beans if you have the forethought – you'll need 240 g (8½ oz) cooked beans.

Chocolate, beetroot and orange cupcakes

Makes 9
Gluten free

400 g (14 oz) tin cannellini (lima) beans, rinsed and drained
3 eggs
½ teaspoon liquid stevia
80 g (2¾ oz) butter, softened
85 g (3 oz/¼ cup) rice malt syrup
1 teaspoon finely grated orange zest
50 g (1¾ oz/½ cup) Dutch-processed cocoa powder
2 teaspoons baking powder
½ teaspoon salt
1 beetroot (beet) (about 175 g/6 oz), peeled and finely grated

Orange mascarpone topping
120 g (4½ oz/½ cup) mascarpone
2 tablespoons thickened (double/heavy) cream
1 teaspoon finely grated orange zest, plus extra shredded zest to garnish
a few drops beetroot (beet) juice (optional)

Preheat the oven to 160°C/320°F (fan-forced) and line a 9-hole 80 ml (2½ fl oz/⅓ cup capacity) muffin tin with paper cases.

Whiz the beans, one of the eggs and the stevia in a food processor until smooth and creamy. Transfer to a bowl and set aside.

Without cleaning the bowl, process the butter, rice malt syrup and zest until smooth and creamy. Add the remaining eggs one at a time, processing well between each addition. Return the bean mixture to the bowl and sift in the cocoa, baking powder and salt, and then process until combined. Stir in the beetroot.

Spoon the mixture into the prepared cases and bake for 20–25 minutes or until a skewer inserted in the centre comes out clean. Remove from the oven and cool for 5 minutes in the tin before removing to a wire rack to cool completely.

Meanwhile, for the orange and mascarpone topping, whisk the mascarpone, cream and zest until slightly thickened. Stir in the beetroot juice (if using). Refrigerate until required.

Spread the cooled cupcakes with the topping and garnish with extra zest.

These cupcakes will keep, un-topped, for 2–3 days in an airtight container. Spread with the topping just before serving.

The simple lime icing is great on these flavoursome cupcakes. If the weather is warm, you may need to chill the coconut oil so that it is solid. Or, if you fancy a chocolaty hit, top them with the Choc avocado mousse (page 76) or the Banana cashew cream (page 33). Soak and cook your own chickpeas if you have the time – you'll need 240 g (8½ oz) cooked chickpeas.

Chai chia cupcakes

Makes 9
Gluten free

420 g (15 oz) tin chickpeas, rinsed and drained
3 eggs
2 teaspoons natural vanilla extract
80 g (2¾ oz) solid virgin coconut oil
85 g (3 oz/¼ cup) rice malt syrup
2 tablespoons coconut flour
1 tablespoon chia seeds
2 teaspoons baking powder
1 teaspoon ground cinnamon, plus extra to sprinkle
1 teaspoon ground cardamom
1 teaspoon ground ginger
½ teaspoon ground star anise

Lime icing
80 g (2¾ oz) solid virgin coconut oil
85 g (3 oz/¼ cup) rice malt syrup
about 1 tablespoon lime juice

Preheat the oven to 160°C/320°F (fan-forced) and line a 9-hole 80 ml (2½ fl oz/⅓ cup capacity) muffin tin with paper cases.

Whiz the chickpeas, one of the eggs and the vanilla in a food processor until smooth and creamy. Transfer to a bowl and set aside.

Without cleaning the bowl, process the coconut oil and rice malt syrup until smooth and creamy. Add the remaining eggs one at a time, processing well between each addition. Return the chickpea mixture to the bowl along with the coconut flour, chia seeds, baking powder and spices, and then process until combined. The batter will look curdled, but don't worry, it will be fine.

Spoon the mixture into the prepared cases and bake for 20–25 minutes or until lightly coloured and just firm to the touch. Remove from the oven and cool for 5 minutes in the tin before removing to a wire rack to cool completely.

For the lime icing, whiz the coconut oil and rice malt syrup in a food processor until smooth and creamy. Do not over-process as the mixture may warm up and melt. Stir in the lime juice a little at a time, tasting as you go until you get the balance of flavour right. If the icing is soft, put it in the refrigerator until ready to use.

Spread the cooled cupcakes with the lime icing and sprinkle with the extra cinnamon. If the weather is warm, keep the iced cakes in the refrigerator until just before serving.

These cupcakes will keep, un-iced for 2–3 days in an airtight container. Spread with the lime icing just before serving.

Peas? Yes, really! We use lots of vegetables and fruits to add natural
sweetness to our baking, so why not peas? They are unusual, but rather fun,
I think. These donuts are also equally delicious dipped in Chocolate glaze
(page 59) or spread with Choc avocado mousse (page 76). Garnish with frozen
peas for added texture if you like.

Baked vanilla & pea donuts

Makes 12

300 g (10½ oz/2 cups) plain (all-purpose) flour
1 tablespoon baking powder
140 g (5 oz/1 cup) frozen green peas, thawed, plus extra to garnish
125 ml (4 fl oz/½ cup) full-cream (whole) milk
100 g (3½ oz) butter, melted, plus extra for greasing
100 g (3½ oz/⅓ cup) Apple purée (page 162)
2 eggs
1 teaspoon natural vanilla extract
1 teaspoon liquid stevia
1 tablespoon slivered pistachios

Avocado coconut icing
1 ripe avocado, seeded and chopped
1 tablespoon coconut powder
1 teaspoon freshly squeezed lime juice, plus extra if required

Preheat the oven to 160°C/320°F (fan-forced). Generously grease two 6-hole 80 ml (2½ fl oz/⅓ cup)
capacity donut tins with the extra melted butter. (If you don't have two, don't worry, they will be fine
cooked in two batches.)

Sift the flour and baking powder together into a large bowl. Make a well in the centre and add the peas,
milk, butter, apple purée, eggs, vanilla and stevia, and then stir until combined.

Put the batter in a piping bag fitted with a 1.5 cm (½ in) plain nozzle (or use a large sealable plastic bag
with the corner snipped off) and pipe the mixture into the prepared donut holes (alternatively, you can
spoon the batter in). Fill each hole about two-thirds full.

Bake for 12–15 minutes or until well-risen and a skewer inserted in the centre comes out clean.
Remove from the oven and set aside to cool in the tin for 5 minutes. Carefully loosen the donuts and
turn onto a wire rack to cool completely.

For the avocado coconut icing, mash and stir the avocado until smooth. Add the coconut powder and lime
juice and mix well. Add a little more lime juice to adjust the flavour balance and consistency if you like.

Spread the cooled donuts with the icing and sprinkle with the pistachios and extra peas. Serve immediately.

Donut moulds come in trays to make 6 donuts – if you don't have two trays, these are fine to cook in two batches. If you don't have donut tins, you can bake these – as well as the other donut recipes on pages 59 and 64 – in a couple of standard muffin tins; they just won't be donuts!

Spiced pumpkin donuts

Makes 12–14

melted butter, for greasing
380 g (13½ oz/1½ cups) steamed and mashed pumpkin (squash), cooled
150 g (5½ oz/½ cup) Apple purée (page 162)
3 eggs
80 ml (2½ fl oz/⅓ cup) macadamia oil or melted butter
1½ teaspoons mixed spice
¼ teaspoon liquid stevia (optional)
225 g (8 oz/1½ cups) plain (all-purpose) flour
2 teaspoons baking powder
pinch salt

Spice powder
40 g (1½ oz/¼ cup) dextrose
2 teaspoons mixed spice
½ teaspoon freshly grated nutmeg

Preheat the oven to 160°C/320°F (fan-forced). Generously grease two 6-hole 80 ml (2½ fl oz/⅓ cup) capacity donut tins with the melted butter. (If you don't have two, don't worry, they will be fine cooked in two batches.)

Beat the pumpkin, apple purée, eggs, oil or butter, mixed spice and stevia (if using) with an electric mixer until smooth. Sift the flour, baking powder and salt together and stir into the pumpkin mixture until just combined.

Put the batter in a piping bag fitted with a 1.5 cm (½ in) plain nozzle (or use a large sealable plastic bag with the corner snipped off) and pipe the mixture into the prepared donut holes (alternatively, you can spoon the batter in). Fill each hole about two-thirds full.

Bake for 10–12 minutes or until well-risen and a skewer inserted in the centre comes out clean. Remove from the oven and set aside to cool in the tin for 5 minutes. Carefully loosen the donuts and turn onto a wire rack.

While the donuts are still warm (but no longer fragile), gently toss them with the combined spice powder ingredients.

These donuts are best served warm from the oven, but will keep for 2–3 days stored in an airtight container.

Left to right
**Baked vanilla
& pea donuts;
Spiced pumpkin donuts**

The buttermilk in conjunction with the bicarbonate of soda helps to give these scones an extra lift. If you don't have buttermilk, you can substitute regular milk mixed with 1 teaspoon of apple cider vinegar.

Chocolate, pistachio & cardamom scones

Makes about 10
Gluten free

225 g (8 oz/1½ cups) gluten-free plain (all-purpose) flour
1 tablespoon baking powder
1½ teaspoons ground cardamom
1 teaspoon xanthan gum
½ teaspoon bicarbonate of soda (baking soda)
60 g (2 oz) cold butter, chopped, plus extra butter to serve
100 g (3½ oz) dark chocolate (70–85% cocoa solids), chopped into chunks
45 g (1½ oz/⅓ cup) pistachios, roughly chopped
30 g (1 oz/¼ cup) almond meal
1 egg, plus extra, lightly beaten, to glaze
about 160 ml (5½ fl oz/⅔ cup) buttermilk

Preheat the oven to 180°C/350°F (fan-forced) and line a baking tray with non-stick baking paper.

Sift the flour, baking powder, cardamom, xanthan gum and bicarbonate of soda into a large bowl. Add the butter and use your fingertips to rub it into the flour until the mixture resembles coarse breadcrumbs. (You can do this in a food processor, just don't over-process – you want to retain visible specks of butter.) Stir in the chocolate, pistachios and almond meal.

Whisk the egg and the buttermilk together. Make a well in the centre of the flour and add the buttermilk mixture. Using a butter knife in a cutting action, combine the mixture until it forms a soft sticky dough. Add a little more buttermilk if the mixture seems dry.

Turn the dough onto a lightly floured surface and very gently knead and press the dough together. Using your fingertips, pat the dough out to a square about 3 cm (1¼ in) thick. Trim the edges with a long sharp knife and cut into nine squares. Place the scones onto the prepared tray so they're almost touching. If you wish, gently press the dough offcuts together and cut more scones as necessary. Carefully brush the top of the scones with egg.

Bake for 20–25 minutes or until well-risen, lightly browned and cooked through. Wrap in a clean dish towel to keep warm and soft. Serve with butter.

These scones are best eaten warm from the oven.

Use your favourite combo of seeds to sprinkle over these muffins. I like a mixture of linseeds (flax seeds), sunflower seeds and pepitas (pumpkin seeds). The muffins are best straight from the oven, but reheat quite well in the microwave. For a little extra indulgence, enjoy with a swipe of butter or Raspberry chia jam (page 163).

Spiced apple & cream cheese muffins

Makes 12

150 g (5½ oz/1 cup) plain (all-purpose) flour
100 g (3½ oz/⅔ cup) wholemeal (whole-wheat) flour
55 g (2 oz/⅓ cup) dextrose
3 teaspoons baking powder
2 teaspoons ground cinnamon
2 teaspoons mixed spice
1 large apple (about 200 g/7 oz), cored and chopped with skin on
150 g (5½ oz) cream cheese, roughly chopped
2 eggs
250 ml (8½ fl oz/1 cup) buttermilk
a mixture of your favourite seeds, for sprinkling

Preheat the oven to 180°C/350°F (fan-forced). Lightly grease a 12-hole 80 ml (2½ fl oz/⅓ cup capacity) muffin tin or line with paper cases.

Sift the flours, dextrose, baking powder and spices into a bowl. Return the husks from the wholemeal flour to the sifted mixture, then mix in the apple.

Mash and stir the cream cheese and eggs together with a whisk until roughly combined. (There will be small lumps of cream cheese remaining, which is what you're after). Whisk in the buttermilk, then pour into the flour mixture and stir with a large spoon until just combined. Do not over-mix.

Spoon the batter into the prepared tray and sprinkle with the seeds.

Bake for 15–20 minutes or until muffins spring back when lightly pressed. Remove from the oven and cool for 2 minutes in the tin before carefully removing to a wire rack.

These muffins are best served warm from the oven, however they will keep for 2–3 days in an airtight container in the refrigerator. Reheat before serving.

This hybrid is a cross between a croissant and muffin – flaky pastry formed in a muffin tin. I've used my favourite rough puff pastry with yeast, which is easy to make, but requires a little patience for resting time. All the sweetness comes from the dried fruit in this recipe. These cruffins are probably best made in cooler weather – if it's too hot, the butter will leak from the pastry.

Earl grey & fig cruffins

Makes 12

1 quantity Rough puff pastry (page 164)
1 earl grey tea bag
75 g (2¾ oz) dried figs, sliced
40 g (1½ oz/¼ cup) sultanas (golden raisins)
35 g (1¼ oz/¼ cup) raisins
45 g (1½ oz/⅓ cup) slivered pistachios or almonds, plus extra to garnish

Prepare the rough puff pastry. Lightly grease a 12-hole 80 ml (2½ fl oz/⅓ cup capacity) muffin tin.

Place the tea bag and fruit in a small heatproof bowl. Add just enough boiling water to cover the fruit and set aside to plump for 30 minutes or until cool, stirring occasionally. Drain, reserving the liquid and fruit separately, and set aside.

Divide the pastry dough in half, then, working with half at a time, roll the dough out to a 30 cm x 40 cm (12 in x 15¾ in) rectangle 3 mm–5 mm (⅛ in–¼ in) thick.

Scatter with half of the soaked fruit and half of the nuts, then roll the pastry into a tight scroll from one of the long edges. Using a sharp, well-floured knife, cut the scroll in half lengthways. (This may look and sound strange, but stick with me.) Now, carefully cut each length into three portions, being careful not to spill the fruit everywhere. Take each portion, twist and curl it around into a nest-like shape and nestle it snugly into the prepared tin. Repeat the process with the remaining dough, fruit and nuts. Cover the dough loosely with plastic wrap and place the tray in a cool place for 45–60 minutes or until risen by about one third.

Preheat the oven to 200°C/400°F (fan-forced).

Bake for 15–18 minutes or until the cruffins are well-risen, golden and flaky. Remove from the oven and cool for 2 minutes in the tin before carefully removing to a wire rack. Brush with the reserved earl grey syrup from soaking the fruit, sprinkle with the extra nuts and serve immediately.

These cruffins are best served warm from the oven, however they will keep for 2–3 days in an airtight container in the refrigerator. Reheat before serving.

These fruity buns are reminiscent of hot cross buns, but without the cross — perfect to eat all year round! Allowing 10 minutes resting time after mixing is my favourite trick with yeast dough — it means there's less kneading required.

Sticky fruit buns

Makes 12

300 ml (10 fl oz) full-cream (whole) milk
40 g (1½ oz) butter, chopped, plus extra to serve
1 tablespoon rice malt syrup
500 g (1 lb 2 oz/3⅓ cups) bread or baker's flour, plus extra to dust
80 g (2¾ oz/½ cup) raisins
80 g (2¾ oz/½ cup) sultanas (golden raisins)
85 g (3 oz/½ cup) seeded dried dates, coarsely chopped
2 teaspoons dried yeast
2 teaspoons mixed spice
2 teaspoons ground cinnamon
½ teaspoon salt
1 egg, lightly beaten

Sticky glaze
2 tablespoons rice malt syrup
1 tablespoon boiling water
½ teaspoon mixed spice

Stir the milk, butter and rice malt syrup together in a small saucepan over low heat until melted and combined. Do not boil. Remove from the heat and set aside to cool to lukewarm.

Combine the flour, dried fruit, yeast, spices and salt in a large bowl. Add the lukewarm milk mixture and the egg and stir until combined. Cover and set aside for 10 minutes.

Turn the mixture onto a lightly floured surface and knead for 5 minutes or until quite smooth. Place the dough in a clean bowl. Cover with plastic wrap or a damp dish towel and set aside in a warm place to prove for about 1½ hours or until the dough doubles in size.

Preheat the oven to 180°C/350°F (fan-forced) and line a baking tray with non-stick baking paper.

Turn the dough onto a lightly floured surface. Knead for about 2 minutes or until smooth and elastic. Divide the dough into 12 equal portions. Shape into smooth balls and place on the prepared tray, so they're almost touching. Cover loosely with plastic wrap. Put the tray in a warm place for about 30 minutes or until the dough has risen by about one-third.

Bake for 18–20 minutes or until well-risen and browned.

For the sticky glaze, combine the rice malt syrup, water and mixed spice in a small heatproof bowl. Stir until dissolved. Brush the tops of the warm buns with glaze and serve, with butter, while still warm.

These buns are best eaten the day they were made, however they will keep for 2–3 days in an airtight container. Reheat before serving.

These choux puffs are a fresh take on the traditional version. The chocolate mousse is decadent, yet wholesome, and the caramelised seeds add a lovely crunchy contrast. If the caramelised seeds are a step too far for you, simply dust these beauties with cocoa. They are best assembled close to serving so the pastry does not soften – but are still pretty incredible if made beforehand.

Choc avocado choux puffs

Makes 10–12

Choux puff mixture
60 g (2 oz) butter, chopped
110 g (4 oz/¾ cup) plain (all-purpose) flour
pinch of salt
3 eggs, at room temperature, lightly beaten

Choc avocado mousse
50 g (1¾ oz) fresh (medjool) dates, pitted and roughly chopped
2 bananas, peeled
1 avocado, seeded and peeled
35 g (1¼ oz/⅓ cup) Dutch-processed cocoa powder

Caramelised seeds
2 tablespoons rice malt syrup
1 tablespoon pepitas (pumpkin seeds)
1 tablespoon sesame seeds

Preheat the oven to 180°C/350°F (fan-forced) and line a baking tray with non-stick baking paper.

For the choux puff mixture, put the butter with 180 ml (6 fl oz/¾ cup) water in a small saucepan over medium heat and bring to the boil. Add the flour and salt and stir vigorously over medium heat for 1–2 minutes, or until the mixture leaves the side of the pan and forms a smooth mass.

Transfer the mixture to the bowl of an electric mixer and allow to cool for 2 minutes. Add the egg gradually, beating well between each addition. Stop adding the egg if it seems like the mixture is starting to thin out. The mixture should be thick and glossy.

Drop tablespoonfuls of mixture about 5 cm (2 in) apart on the prepared tray. Splash the tray with a little cold water from your fingertips – this will help create steam in the oven. Bake for 20 minutes, reduce the oven temperature to 160°C/320°F (fan-forced) and bake for a further 5–10 minutes or until the pastry is puffed and golden. Remove from oven, cut in half and remove any soft pastry from the centres. Return to the oven for 5 minutes to dry out. Cool on a wire rack.

Meanwhile, for the choc avocado mousse, put the dates in a small heatproof bowl and cover with warm water. Leave to soak for 10 minutes. Drain and transfer the dates to a food processor with the banana, avocado and cocoa powder. Whiz until smooth. Transfer to a bowl, cover and keep in the refrigerator until needed.

Just before serving, fill the base of each puff with a spoonful of the mousse and top with the lids.

For the caramelised seeds, heat the syrup and seeds in a very small non-stick frying pan over medium heat. Cook, stirring constantly for about 1 minute or until the mixture starts to thicken slightly. Working quickly, spoon a dollop of the mixture over the filled puffs. Leave to set for a few minutes, and then serve immediately.

The pumpkin (squash) adds lightness to these scones that you perhaps wouldn't expect, and the colour is sensational! I am a traditionalist when it comes to making scones and believe you should rub the butter in with your fingertips. You can do this step with a food processor if you like; just don't process for too long as retaining visible specks of butter helps the texture of the scones.

Pumpkin & fennel scones

Makes about 10

225 g (8 oz/1½ cups) plain (all-purpose) flour
3 teaspoons baking powder
30 g (1 oz) cold butter, chopped
2 teaspoons fennel seeds, roughly crushed in a pestle and mortar, plus extra to sprinkle
190 g (6½ oz/¾ cup) steamed and mashed pumpkin (squash), cooled
about 125 ml (4 fl oz/½ cup) buttermilk, plus extra to glaze
butter or Chia raspberry jam (page 163) and cream, to serve

Preheat the oven to 200°C/400°F (fan-forced) and line a baking tray with non-stick baking paper.

Sift the flour and baking powder together into a large bowl. Add the butter and use your fingertips to rub it into the flour until the mixture resembles coarse breadcrumbs. Stir in the fennel seeds.

Make a well in the centre of the flour mixture and add the pumpkin and buttermilk. Using a butter knife in a cutting action, combine the mixture until it forms a soft sticky dough. Add a little more buttermilk if the mixture seems dry.

Turn the dough onto a lightly floured surface and very gently knead and press the dough together. Using your fingertips, pat the dough out to about 3 cm (1¼ in) thick. Cut out the scones using a 5 cm (2 in) round cutter dipped in flour. Place the scones on the prepared tray so they're almost touching. Gently press the dough offcuts together and cut more scones as necessary. Carefully brush the top of the scones with buttermilk and sprinkle with the extra crushed fennel seeds.

Bake for 20–25 minutes or until well-risen, lightly browned and cooked through. Wrap in a clean dish towel to keep warm and soft. Serve with butter or jam and cream.

These scones are best eaten warm from the oven, but will keep for 2–3 days in an airtight container. Split and toast before eating.

For the light kneading process used in this recipe, put a little oil on the clean bench in front of you and smooth it around with your hands to cover a small area. Tip the dough onto the oiled area and knead the dough about 10–12 times only – your job is done – return the dough to the bowl and come back again later. This recipe just requires time, not effort!

Cinnamon, apple & cream cheese scrolls

Makes 12

350 ml (12 fl oz) full-cream (whole) milk
500 g (1 lb 2 oz/3⅓ cups) plain bread or baker's
　flour, plus extra to dust
1 tablespoon rice malt syrup
40 g (1½ oz) chopped butter
2 egg yolks
2 teaspoons dried yeast
1 teaspoon salt
light olive oil, for kneading
butter, to serve (optional)

Filling
150 g (5½ oz) cream cheese, softened
2 teaspoons ground cinnamon
1 egg yolk
1 large granny smith apple
　(about 200 g/7 oz), peeled, cored and
　chopped into 5 mm (¼ in) pieces

Glaze
1 tablespoon rice malt syrup

Whisk the milk, 2 tablespoons of the flour and the rice malt syrup together in a small saucepan over medium heat. Whisking constantly, bring the mixture to the boil. Remove from the heat, transfer to a large bowl, stir in the butter and leave to cool to lukewarm, whisking occasionally to knock the heat out.

Whisk the egg yolk into the lukewarm milk mixture, and then add the remaining flour, yeast and salt. Mix with your hands to form a soft dough. Cover with plastic wrap or a clean damp dish towel and set aside for 10 minutes.

Turn the mixture onto a lightly oiled surface and knead 10–12 times only. Return the dough to the bowl. Cover and set aside in a warm place 1½ hours, giving the dough two more light kneads during this time – one after 30 minutes and one after 60 minutes.

For the filling, beat the cream cheese and cinnamon with an electric mixer until smooth. Add the egg yolk and continue to beat until the mixture is combined and of a spreading consistency.

Preheat the oven to 180°C/350°F (fan-forced) and line a baking tray with non-stick baking paper.

Turn the dough onto a lightly floured surface and, without knocking all the air out of it, gently roll out to a 30 cm x 40 cm (12 in x 15¾ in) rectangle. Gently spread the cheese mixture over the dough and sprinkle with apple. Roll up firmly from one long edge and cut into twelve even slices with a sharp knife. Lay the slices flat on the prepared tray so they're almost touching and cover loosely. Put the tray in a warm place for about 30 minutes or until the dough has risen by about one-third.

Bake for 15 minutes, then turn down the heat to 160°C/320°F (fan-forced) and bake for a further 10–12 minutes, or until well-risen and browned.

For the glaze, combine the syrup and 1 tablespoon boiling water in a small heatproof bowl. Brush the tops of the warm buns with glaze and serve while still warm.

These buns are best eaten the day they were made, however they will keep for 2–3 days in an airtight container. Reheat before serving.

These little galettes make a rather posh afternoon tea. The amaretto in the filling is optional, but it does give it a bit of an edge. An orange liqueur would work very well too. If you find you need to re-roll the pastry, stack the pastry scraps on top of each other rather than scrunching them together. This way you'll maintain the layers that you have worked so hard to create.

Chocolate pear frangipane galettes

Makes 6
Can be made gluten free

½ quantity Rough puff pastry (page 164) or Gluten-free rough puff pastry (page 165)
2 beurre bosc or corella pears
1 tablespoon lemon juice
1 tablespoon rice malt syrup, warmed
crème fraîche or creamy natural yoghurt, to serve

Frangipane
100 g (3½ oz) butter, softened
2 tablespoons rice malt syrup
2 egg yolks
120 g (4½ oz/1 cup) almond meal
2 tablespoons cornflour (cornstarch)
35 g (1¼ oz/⅓ cup) Dutch-processed cocoa powder
2 tablespoons amaretto (optional)

Preheat the oven to 180°C/350°F (fan-forced) and line two baking trays with non-stick baking paper.

Roll out the pastry on a lightly floured surface to about 3 mm (⅛ in) thick. Cut six 14 cm (5½ in) circles from the pastry. (I use a small upturned bowl as my guide to cut a template from card. Be careful not to squish the edges of the dough together as you don't want to impede the rise.) Gently transfer the circles to the prepared trays.

Bake for 10–15 minutes or until puffed and starting to brown. You should have lots of lovely flaky layers. Remove from the oven and use a clean dish towel to gently press the pastry to flatten it slightly. Set aside for 15 minutes to cool.

Meanwhile, to make the frangipane, beat the butter and rice malt syrup with an electric mixer until pale and creamy, scraping down the sides of the bowl as necessary. Add the egg yolk and beat until combined. Sift the almond meal, cornflour and cocoa into the butter mixture, and then mix on low speed until combined. Stir in the amaretto (if using).

Divide the frangipane mixture between the pastry circles and spread out evenly, leaving a 1 cm (½ in) border around the edge. Core and slice the pears very thinly and brush them with lemon juice to stop them browning. Arrange the slices on the galettes so they are slightly overlapping. Bake for 15–18 minutes or until pears begin to curl and the pastry is a deep golden colour. Remove from the oven and set aside to cool on a wire rack. Brush with the warmed rice malt syrup. Serve warm or at room temperature with a dollop of crème fraîche or yoghurt.

Traditionally, madeleines are enjoyed warm from the oven. These not-so-traditional madeleines are equally delicious warm or cool. They keep well for a day or two. Soak and cook your own cannellini (lima) beans if you have the forethought — you'll need 240 g (8½ oz) cooked beans. If you only have one madeleine tray, don't worry, the mixture will hold between cooking batches.

Almond, mandarin & orange blossom madeleines

Makes about 20
Gluten free

melted butter, for greasing
400 g (14 oz) tin cannellini (lima) beans, rinsed and drained
3 eggs
80 g (2¾ oz) butter, softened
85 g (3 oz/¼ cup) rice malt syrup
2 teaspoons vanilla bean paste
2 teaspoons finely grated mandarin zest
60 g (2 oz/½ cup) almond meal
2 teaspoons baking powder
2 teaspoons orange blossom water
dextrose, to dust (optional)

Preheat the oven to 160°C/320°F (fan-forced). Generously brush two madeleine trays with melted butter.

Whiz the cannellini beans and one of the eggs in a food processor until creamy. Transfer to a bowl and set aside.

Without cleaning the processor bowl, process the butter, rice malt syrup, vanilla and zest until smooth and creamy. Add the remaining eggs one at a time, processing well between each addition. Return the cannellini bean mixture to the processor with the almond meal, baking powder and orange blossom water, and then process until combined. The batter may look curdled, but don't worry, it will be fine.

Spoon about 1 tablespoon of the mixture into each hole of the prepared tray and bake for 13–15 minutes or until just firm to the touch and browning around the edges. Remove from the oven and cool for 5 minute before transferring to a wire rack to cool completely. Dust with dextrose if you like.

These madeleines are delicious served warm, however they will keep for 1–2 days in an airtight container.

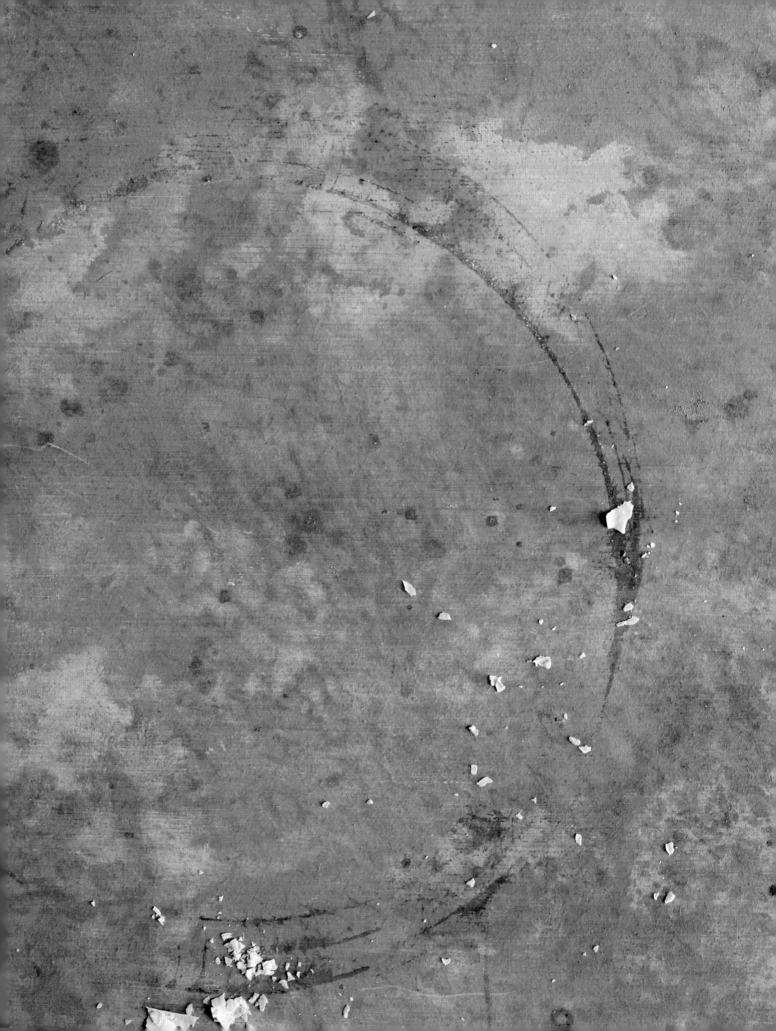

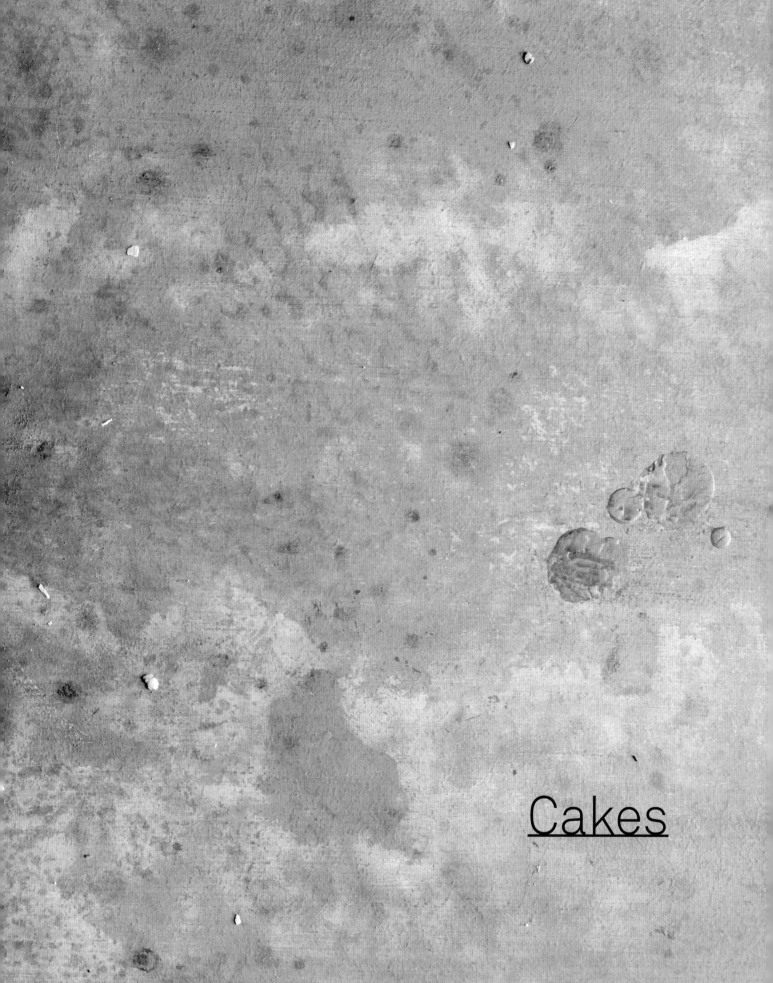

Cakes

'Chocolate cake' might be a bit of an understatement for this cake. Who would have imagined that a cake made with legumes could ever be this light and tasty? This cake has a sophisticated bitterness to it – just add a little more stevia if you would like a sweeter version. Soak and cook your own kidney beans if you have the time – you'll need 480 g (1 lb 1 oz) cooked beans.

Chocolate cake

Serves 10–12
Gluten free

melted butter, for greasing
100 g (3½ oz/1 cup) Dutch-processed cocoa powder, plus extra for dusting
2 teaspoons baking powder
½ teaspoon salt
2 x 420 g (15 oz) tins kidney beans, rinsed and drained
6 eggs
1 tablespoon natural vanilla extract
½–1 teaspoon liquid stevia (optional)
150 g (5½ oz) butter, softened
170 g (6 oz/½ cup) rice malt syrup
creamy natural yoghurt or crème fraîche, to serve

Preheat the oven to 160°C/320°F (fan-forced). Grease a 22 cm (8¾ in) baba or ring (or 20 cm/8 in round) tin generously with melted butter. Add a little of the extra cocoa powder to the cake tin, tilt the tin to cover the butter with the cocoa powder, then tip out the excess.

Combine the cocoa powder, baking powder and salt in a small bowl and set aside.

Whiz the beans, 1 egg, the vanilla extract and stevia (if using) in a food processor until smooth and creamy. Transfer to a bowl and set aside.

Without cleaning the processor bowl, process the butter and rice malt syrup until smooth and creamy. Add the remaining eggs one at a time, processing well between each addition. Return the bean mixture to the processor and sift in the cocoa, baking powder and salt. Process until well combined.

Pour the mixture into the prepared tin and bake for 40–45 minutes or until a skewer inserted into the centre comes out clean. Remove from the oven and leave to cool for 10 minutes before turning out onto a wire rack to cool completely. Serve, dusted with extra cocoa if you like and a dollop of yoghurt or crème fraîche.

This cake will keep for 2–3 days in an airtight container.

This is a classic almond cake with a mandarin twist. If mandarins are out of season, by all means substitute two oranges, although they will need about two hours to pre-cook. The mandarins or oranges can be cooked the day before you need them.

Almond mandarin cake

Serves 10–12
Gluten free

400 g (14 oz) mandarins (about 4 small), unpeeled
270 g (9½ oz/1⅔ cups) natural almonds
1 teaspoon baking powder
6 eggs
115 g (4 oz/⅓ cup) rice malt syrup
½ teaspoon orange blossom water
dextrose, for dusting (optional)

Put the mandarins in a small saucepan, cover with cold water and bring to the boil. Simmer for 45 minutes or until very tender, topping up with water as necessary. Drain, cool to room temperature, cut in half and remove any pips.

Preheat the oven to 140°C/275°F (fan-forced). Grease a 23 cm (9 in) springform cake tin and line the base with non-stick baking paper.

Whiz the almonds in a food processor until finely ground. Transfer to a large bowl and stir in the baking powder.

In the same food processor bowl, process the cooled mandarins and the eggs and rice malt syrup until well combined and frothy. Add to the almond meal mixture along with the orange blossom water and mix until well combined.

Pour the cake batter into the prepared tin and bake for 50–55 minutes or until a skewer inserted into the centre comes out clean. Remove from the oven and leave to cool for 15 minutes before transferring to a wire rack to cool completely. Dust with dextrose, if desired, just before serving.

This cake will keep for 2–3 days in an airtight container.

The sweet potato gives this cake a slight sweetness, great texture and helps to keep it moist. You can serve it with the Lime syrup on page 97 if you like, but I quite like it as it comes, or with a dollop of creamy Greek-style yoghurt on the side.

Sweet potato, lime & poppy seed cake

Serves 10–12

1 orange sweet potato (about 400 g/14 oz), peeled and chopped
225 g (8 oz/1½ cups) plain (all-purpose) flour, plus extra for dusting
3 teaspoons baking powder
40 g (1½ oz/¼ cup) poppy seeds
125 g (4½ oz) butter, softened
80 g (2¾ oz/½ cup) dextrose, plus extra for dusting (optional)
1½ teaspoons finely grated lime zest
3 eggs
180 ml (6 fl oz/¾ cup) buttermilk

Steam or microwave the sweet potato until tender. Drain, mash and set aside to cool. You will need 260 g (9oz/1 cup) sweet potato for this cake.

Preheat the oven to 160°C/320°F (fan-forced). Grease a 22 cm (8¾ in) baba or ring (or 20 cm/8 in round or heart) tin generously. Add a little flour to the cake tin, tilt the tin to cover the inside with the flour, then tip out the excess.

Sift the flour and baking powder into a large bowl. Stir in the poppy seeds. Set aside.

Beat the butter, dextrose and lime zest with an electric mixer until pale and fluffy, scraping down the side of the bowl, as necessary. Add the eggs one at a time, beating well between each addition, then stir in the sweet potato. In two batches, stir in the flour mixture and buttermilk until just combined.

Spread the mixture into the prepared tin and bake for 25–30 minutes or until a skewer inserted into the centre comes out clean. Remove from the oven and leave to cool for 2 minutes before turning out onto a wire rack to cool completely. Serve, dusted with extra dextrose if you like.

This cake will keep for 2–3 days in an airtight container.

I love that all the sweetness in this moist and tender cake comes from the fruit, so you don't even need a replacement for sugar. I keep a stock of overripe bananas in my freezer for baking — when they've gone past the point of no return for eating, peel and place in a sealed container and pop them into the freezer. They'll keep for 4–6 weeks.

Hummingbird cake

Serves 16

265 g (9½ oz/2¾ cups) plain (all-purpose) flour
1 tablespoon baking powder
2 teaspoons ground cinnamon
440 g (15½ oz) tin crushed pineapple in natural juice
2 large overripe bananas, mashed
100 g (3½ oz/⅓ cup) Apple purée (page 162)
60 ml (2 fl oz/¼ cup) fresh passionfruit pulp (about 3 plump passionfruit)
2 eggs
150 g (5½ oz) butter, melted
20 g (¾ oz/⅓ cup) flaked coconut, for sprinkling

Preheat the oven to 160°C/320°F (fan-forced). Grease a 20 cm x 30 cm (8 in x 12 in) shallow cake tin and line the base with non-stick baking paper.

Sift the flour, baking powder and cinnamon into a large bowl. Set aside.

Drain the pineapple – you can save the juice for another purpose. Combine the pineapple, banana, apple, passionfruit pulp and eggs in a large bowl. Stir in the butter and the flour mixture until just combined.

Spread the mixture into the prepared tin and sprinkle over the coconut. Bake for 30–35 minutes or until a skewer inserted into the centre comes out clean.

Remove from the oven and leave to cool for 10 minutes before gently turning out onto a wire rack to cool completely, coconut-side up.

This cake will keep for 2–3 days in an airtight container.

I know this is another chocolate cake, but it is quite different from the one on page 88, which has a more fudgy texture. This version is a little lighter but no less delicious. You'll notice the icing on this cake has a slightly grainy appearance. This is because the size of the dextrose crystals is not as fine as icing sugar. You can blend the dextrose to make it finer, if you like.

Everyday chocolate cake

Serves about 20

250 g (9 oz) butter, chopped
200 g (7 oz) dark chocolate (70–85% cocoa solids)
115 g (4 oz/⅓ cup) rice malt syrup
150 g (5½ oz/1 cup) plain (all-purpose) flour
50 g (1¾ oz/½ cup) cocoa powder (unsweetened)
2 teaspoons baking powder
¼ teaspoon bicarbonate of soda (baking soda)
150 g (5½ oz/½ cup) Apple purée (page 162)
3 eggs
125 ml (4 fl oz/½ cup) buttermilk

Chocolate icing
100 g (3½ oz) butter, softened
240 g (8½ oz/1½ cups) dextrose
25 g (1 oz/¼ cup) Dutch-processed cocoa powder
80 ml (2½ fl oz/⅓ cup) milk

Preheat the oven to 160°C/320°F (fan-forced). Grease two 20 cm (8 in) sandwich (shallow) tins and line the bases with non-stick baking paper.

Melt the butter, chocolate and rice malt syrup in a medium saucepan over low heat, stirring occasionally.

Sift the flour, cocoa powder, baking powder and bicarbonate of soda into a bowl and set aside.

Whisk the apple purée into the cooled chocolate mixture, followed by the eggs and then the buttermilk. Add the flour mixture and stir until combined.

Divide the mixture evenly between the prepared tins and bake for 18–20 minutes or until a skewer inserted into the centre comes out clean. Remove from the oven and leave to cool for 10 minutes before turning out onto a wire rack to cool completely.

For the chocolate icing, beat the butter with an electric mixer until pale, light and fluffy. Sift together the dextrose and cocoa powder. Add half of this mixture to the butter, and beat until well combined. Slowly add the milk and the remaining dextrose mixture, beating until the icing is light and fluffy. Add a little more milk if required, to get a spreadable consistency.

Put one cake on a serving plate and spread just under half of the chocolate icing on top. Place the remaining cake on top of the icing and cover with the remaining icing. Smooth around the sides of the cake with a palette knife, if you like.

This cake will keep for 2–3 days in an airtight container.

The coconut and lime in this simple cake gives it a distinctively tropical feel — which will keep you coming back for more!

Coconut cake with lime syrup

Serves 10–12

150 g (5½ oz/1 cup) plain (all-purpose) flour
90 g (3 oz/1 cup) desiccated (dried shredded) coconut
2 teaspoons baking powder
4 eggs
125 ml (4 fl oz/½ cup) coconut milk
100 g (3½ oz/⅓ cup) Apple purée (page 162)
50 g (1¾ oz) butter, melted
½ teaspoon liquid stevia
pinch of salt
creamy natural yoghurt or cream, to serve

Lime syrup
85 g (3 oz/¼ cup) rice malt syrup
125 ml (4 fl oz/½ cup) freshly squeezed lime juice

Preheat the oven to 160°C/320°F (fan-forced). Grease a deep 18 cm (7 in) cake tin and line the base with non-stick baking paper.

Combine the flour, desiccated coconut and baking powder in a large mixing bowl. Separate two of the eggs and put the whites in the bowl of an electric mixer and set aside. In another bowl, whisk the yolks, remaining eggs, coconut milk, apple purée, butter and stevia together and set aside.

Beat the egg whites with the salt just until firm peaks form. Fold half of the egg white and all of the liquid ingredients into the dry ingredients until combined. Add the remaining egg white and gently fold into the mixture until combined. Pour into the prepared tin and spread evenly.

Bake for 35–40 minutes or until a skewer inserted into the centre comes out clean. Remove from the oven and leave to cool for 5 minutes before transferring to a serving plate with a rim.

For the lime syrup, combine the rice malt syrup, lime juice and 1 tablespoon water in a small bowl and stir until the syrup dissolves. Poke lots of holes in the cake with a skewer and slowly pour about half of the syrup over the cake.

Serve warm or cold with a dollop of creamy yoghurt or cream on the side and the remaining syrup.

This cake will keep for 2–3 days in an airtight container.

left to right
**Everyday chocolate
cake; Coconut cake
with lime syrup**

This is a great way to use up bananas that are past their best. I like to slice this loaf, pop small squares of baking paper between the slices to stop them sticking together and freeze them in a sealed container. My eldest son is a particular fan of this cake. He loves it for school lunches.

Seeded banana & pear loaf

Serves 10–12

170 g (6 oz/½ cup) rice malt syrup
125 ml (4 fl oz/½ cup) natural yoghurt
2 eggs
50 g (1¾ oz) butter, melted
2 teaspoons natural vanilla extract
2 ripe bananas, mashed
1 pear (about 230 g/8 oz), unpeeled and grated
300 g (10½ oz/2 cups) plain (all-purpose) flour
3 teaspoons baking powder
½ teaspoon bicarbonate of soda (baking soda)
1 tablespoon sunflower seeds
1 tablespoon pepitas (pumpkin seeds)
extra butter, to serve (optional)

Preheat the oven to 160°C/320°F (fan-forced). Grease a loaf (bar) tin (11.5 cm x 21.5 cm/4½ in x 8½ in; 1.25 litre/42 fl oz capacity) and line the base and two long sides with a piece of non-stick baking paper, extending the paper about 4 cm (1½ in) above the sides of the tin to assist with the removal of the cooked loaf.

Whisk the rice malt syrup, yoghurt, eggs, butter and vanilla extract together in a large mixing bowl. Stir in the banana and pear. Sift the flour, baking powder and bicarbonate of soda over the mixture and stir until just combined.

Spoon the mixture into the prepared tin, smooth the surface and sprinkle with the seeds. Bake for 60–65 minutes or until a skewer inserted into the centre comes out clean. Remove from the oven and cool for 5 minutes before transferring to a wire rack to cool completely. Serve with extra butter if you like.

This cake will keep for 2–3 days in an airtight container.

You will need at least five mandarins for this recipe — make sure you keep
two of them whole, for slicing. This cake is beautifully moist with slightly
savoury, grassy notes from the olive oil and bay leaves, and freshness from
the mandarin. If mandarins are out of season, this cake works perfectly well
with oranges, blood oranges or meyer lemons.

Mandarin & bay leaf olive oil loaf

Serves 10

160 ml (5½ fl oz/⅔ cup) mild extra-virgin olive oil
4 fresh bay leaves, crumpled/bruised, plus extra to decorate
5–6 mandarins (about 600 g/1 lb 5 oz), depending on their size
225 g (8 oz/1½ cups) plain (all-purpose) flour
2 teaspoons baking powder
¼ teaspoon bicarbonate of soda (baking soda)
¼ teaspoon salt
100 g (3½ oz/⅓ cup) Apple purée (page 162)
80 ml (2½ fl oz/⅓ cup) buttermilk
3 eggs

Heat the olive oil and bay leaves in a small saucepan over low heat for about 10 minutes or until bubbles start to form around the leaves. Set aside to cool and infuse, about 30 minutes. Remove and discard the bay leaves, reserving the oil.

Finely zest and juice 3 mandarins — you need 2 teaspoons of zest and 80 ml (2½ fl oz/⅓ cup) juice. Thinly slice the remaining whole unpeeled mandarins. Set aside.

Preheat the oven to 160°C/320°F (fan-forced). Grease a loaf (bar) tin (11.5 cm x 21.5 cm/4½ in x 8½ in; 1.25 litre/42 fl oz capacity) and line the base and two long sides with a piece of non-stick baking paper, extending the paper about 4 cm (1½ in) above the sides of the tin to assist with the removal of the cooked loaf.

Sift the flour, baking powder, bicarbonate of soda and salt into a large bowl. Set aside.

Whisk the cooled olive oil, apple purée, mandarin zest and juice, buttermilk and eggs together in a large mixing bowl. Add the flour mixture and stir until combined. Pour into the prepared tin and top with the mandarin slices, slightly overlapping them along the centre, as they will spread out as the cake rises.

Bake for 45–50 minutes or until a skewer inserted into the centre comes out clean. Remove from the oven and leave to cool for 5 minutes before gently turning out onto a wire rack to cool completely, mandarin-side up.

This cake will keep for 2–3 days in an airtight container.

The combination of the vegetables and the coconut flour gives this cake a unique, surprisingly light, texture. It's important to note that coconut flours can vary in the amount of moisture they absorb – so, I suggest you add the flour in the ingredients list, then wait a couple of minutes to see if you need to add a little more.

Carrot, parsnip & cardamom loaf

Serves 12
Gluten free

6 eggs
140 g (5 oz/½ cup) Apple purée (page 162)
85 g (3 oz/¼ cup) rice malt syrup
2 teaspoons natural vanilla extract
2 teaspoons ground cinnamon
2 teaspoons ground cardamom
½ teaspoon salt
125 ml (4 fl oz/½ cup) melted virgin coconut oil
2 carrots (about 240 g/8½ oz), finely grated
1 small parsnip (about 120 g/4½ oz), finely grated
about 50 g (1¾ oz/⅓ cup) coconut flour
150 g (5½ oz/1 cup) seeded dried dates, chopped
1 teaspoon bicarbonate of soda (baking soda)
2 teaspoons apple cider vinegar
2 tablespoons flaked coconut, for sprinkling
butter or whipped solid virgin coconut oil, to serve (optional)

Preheat the oven to 160°C/320°F (fan-forced). Grease a loaf (bar) tin (11.5 cm x 21.5 cm/4½ in x 8½ in; 1.25 litre/42 fl oz capacity) and line the base and two long sides with a piece of non-stick baking paper, extending the paper about 4 cm (1½ in) above the sides of the tin to assist with the removal of the cooked loaf.

Whisk the eggs, apple purée, rice malt syrup, vanilla extract, spices and salt together in a large mixing bowl. Add the coconut oil and whisk well, then stir in the grated carrot and parsnip.

Add the coconut flour and mix until combined. Set aside to sit for 2 minutes to give the coconut flour a chance to thicken. The mixture should be quite thick and drop heavily from the spoon. Add a little more flour if the mixture seems too wet.

Stir in the dates and bicarbonate of soda, and then finally, working quickly, stir in the apple cider vinegar.

Spoon the mixture into the prepared tin and sprinkle over the coconut. Bake for 1 hour 15 minutes – 1 hour 20 minutes or until a skewer inserted into the centre comes out clean. Remove from the oven and cool for 10 minutes before turning out onto a wire rack to cool completely.

This cake will keep for 2–3 days in an airtight container.

The nuttiness and extra flavour that comes from browned butter is fantastic. Just don't walk away from the pan as those delicious milk solids will change from toasty-brown to nearly burnt in the blink of an eye.

Brown butter loaf with brown butter frosting

Serves 10

125 g (4½ oz) butter
170 g (6 oz/½ cup) rice malt syrup
small handful hazelnuts
150 g (5½ oz/1 cup) plain (all-purpose) flour
90 g (3 oz/¾ cup) almond meal
2 teaspoons baking powder
3 eggs
1 tablespoon natural vanilla extract
pinch of salt

Brown butter frosting
100 g (3½ oz) butter
100 g (3½ oz) cream cheese, softened
2 tablespoons rice malt syrup
1 teaspoon natural vanilla extract
pinch of salt

Preheat the oven to 160°C/320°F (fan-forced). Line a baking tray with non-stick baking paper. Grease a small loaf (bar) tin (11.5 cm x 21.5 cm/4½ in x 8½ in; 1.25 litre/42 fl oz capacity) and line the base and two long sides with a piece of non-stick baking paper extending the paper about 4 cm (1½ in) above the sides of the tin to assist with the removal of the cooked loaf.

Heat the butter in a small saucepan over low heat until the butter melts and the milk solids (the little specks that separate from the liquid portion of the butter) become golden brown and give off a delicious nutty aroma. Swirl the pan so you can see the colour of the solids through the foam. Remove from the heat immediately and dunk the base of the pan in a sink of cold water to stop the cooking process. Whisk in the rice malt syrup and set the pan aside for the mixture to cool to room temperature – it should still be liquid.

Spread the hazelnuts over the prepared baking tray and bake for 5–8 minutes or until fragrant and the skins have loosened. Let the nuts cool slightly then rub them in a clean dish towel to remove the skins. Discard the skins and roughly chop the nuts. Sift the flour, almond meal and baking powder into a large bowl. Set aside.

Beat the eggs and vanilla extract with an electric mixer until frothy. Add the salt, and then continue to beat until the mixture is very thick and creamy – the mixture should leave a ribbon trail across the surface. Depending on your mixer, this could take up to 10 minutes. While still beating, gradually add the butter mixture.

Gently fold in the sifted flour mixture in two batches. Pour into the prepared tin and bake for 35–40 minutes or until a skewer inserted into the centre comes out clean. Remove from the oven and leave to cool for 5 minutes before turning out onto a wire rack to cool completely.

For the brown butter frosting, brown the butter as directed above. Pour into a small bowl and refrigerate until set. Beat the solidified butter with an electric mixer until pale and creamy. Add the cream cheese, rice malt syrup, vanilla extract and salt and beat until smooth and fluffy.

Spread the cooled cake with the frosting and sprinkle over the hazelnuts.

This cake will keep for 2–3 days in an airtight container.

This cheesecake is perfect for peanut fans, with its peanut butter swirl and chocolaty peanut base. Make sure you give the peanut butter a good stir before measuring it out, as the oil and peanuts tend to separate in natural peanut butter.

Peanut butter swirl cheesecake

Serves 10–12
Gluten free

500 g (1 lb 2 oz) cream cheese, softened
2 tablespoons rice malt syrup
½ teaspoon liquid stevia (optional)
190 g (6½ oz/⅔ cup) natural crunchy peanut butter
60 ml (2 fl oz/¼ cup) coconut milk
2 eggs
2 tablespoons salted roasted peanuts

Base
150 g (5½ oz/1 cup) salted roasted peanuts
115 g (4 oz/1½ cups) shredded coconut
2 tablespoons Dutch-processed cocoa powder
2 tablespoons rice malt syrup
30 g (1 oz) butter, melted

Grease a 23 cm (9 in) springform cake tin and line the base with non-stick baking paper.

For the base, whiz the peanuts and shredded coconut in a food processor until you have a coarse sand-like texture. Add the remaining ingredients and process until combined and the mixture clings together when pressed with your fingertips. Press the mixture firmly and evenly into the prepared tin, and pop it in the refrigerator until required.

Preheat the oven to 140°C/275°F (fan-forced).

Beat the cream cheese, rice malt syrup, stevia (if using) and half of the peanut butter (reserving the remaining peanut butter to swirl through the top) with an electric mixer until smooth. Add the coconut milk and beat again until combined. Add the eggs one at a time, beating well between each addition. Pour the mixture over the cheesecake base.

Gently soften the remaining peanut butter in a small pan over low heat or in the microwave. Place dollops of peanut butter on top of the cheesecake and swirl it through the cheese mixture with the tip of a small knife. Sprinkle over the peanuts.

Bake for 25–30 minutes or until the centre is just set – it should wobble slightly. Turn off the oven and leave to cool with the door closed for 1 hour. Chill in the refrigerator for 3 hours or overnight. Remove from the tin and place on a serving plate.

This cheesecake will keep for 2–3 days, covered, in the refrigerator.

This crustless cheesecake is a real treat with few ingredients. The cookies crumbled over the top add a great crunch and the blueberries add a touch of sweetness. You can also use fruits such as cherries or raspberries instead of the blueberries.

Cookies & cream blueberry cheesecake

Serves 12–16
Gluten free

500 g (1 lb 2 oz) cream cheese, softened
2 teaspoons vanilla bean paste
½ teaspoon liquid stevia
2 eggs
80 g (2¾ oz/⅓ cup) sour cream
3 teaspoons cornflour (cornstarch)
5 Cacao nib hazelnut cookies (page 19), broken into chunks
125 g (4½ oz) fresh or frozen blueberries

Preheat the oven to 140°C/275°F (fan-forced). Grease and line the base and two long sides of a 17 cm x 26 cm (6¾ in x 10¼ in) slice tin with a piece of non-stick baking paper, extending the paper about 4 cm (1½ in) above the sides of the tin to assist with the removal of the cooked cheesecake.

Whiz the cream cheese, vanilla bean paste and stevia in a food processor until smooth. Add the eggs, sour cream and cornflour and process until well combined.

Pour the mixture into the prepared tin and sprinkle over the cookie chunks and blueberries. Bake for 30–35 minutes, or until the top is lightly browned and the centre is just set – it should wobble slightly. Chill in the refrigerator for 2 hours or until ready to serve.

This cheesecake will keep for 2–3 days, covered, in the refrigerator.

Left to right
**Peanut butter swirl
cheesecake;
Cookies & cream
blueberry cheesecake**

The base for this light and summery tart can be made a couple of days in advance and stored in an airtight container. You can fill the base 3–4 hours before serving. Use any berries or summer fruits that are in season.

Lime cheesecake tart

Serves 8
Gluten free

125 ml (4 fl oz/½ cup) thickened (double/heavy) cream
250 g (9 oz) cream cheese, softened
2 tablespoons rice malt syrup
2 teaspoons finely grated lime zest
2 tablespoons freshly squeezed lime juice
2 egg whites
pinch of salt
250 g (9 oz) fresh strawberries, sliced
mint leaves, to serve

Base
150 g (5½ oz/1 cup) sunflower seeds
115 g (4 oz/1½ cups) shredded coconut
2 tablespoons sesame seeds
2 tablespoons rice malt syrup
1 tablespoon melted virgin coconut oil
1 teaspoon ground ginger
1 egg white
¼ teaspoon liquid stevia (optional)
pinch of salt

Preheat the oven to 140°C/275°F (fan-forced).

For the base, whiz the sunflower seeds and shredded coconut in a food processor until you have a coarse sand-like texture. Add the remaining base ingredients and process until combined and the mixture clings together when pressed with your fingertips. Press the mixture firmly into a 12 cm x 35 cm (4¾ in x 13¾ in) rectangular loose-based fluted tart tin, evenly covering the base and sides. Bake for 15–20 minutes or until lightly browned. Remove from the oven and set aside to cool completely.

Whip the cream with an electric mixer until soft peaks form. Transfer to a bowl. Beat the cream cheese, rice malt syrup, lime zest and juice until smooth. Transfer to another bowl and fold in the whipped cream.

Give the bowl for the electric mixer a good clean and beat the egg whites and salt until soft peaks form. Gently fold into the cream cheese mixture in two batches.

Spoon the cheesecake mixture into the cooled base and refrigerate until serving. Serve topped with the strawberries and mint.

This tart will keep for 1–2 days, covered, in the refrigerator.

Baked cheesecake is one of my all-time favourite desserts. The ricotta cheese adds lightness and the dates add a subtle sweetness.

Baked lemon cheesecake

Serves 10–12
Gluten free

1 quantity Almond pastry crust (page 153)
100 g (3½ oz) fresh (medjool) dates, pitted and roughly chopped
350 g (12½ oz) fresh firm ricotta cheese
350 g (12½ oz) cream cheese, softened
3 eggs, separated
1 tablespoon finely grated lemon zest, plus extra shredded zest to serve
60 ml (2 fl oz/¼ cup) freshly squeezed lemon juice
1 vanilla bean, seeds scraped
1½ tablespoons cornflour (cornstarch)
pinch of salt
figs, fresh berries or other fruits in season, for decorating
rice malt syrup, to drizzle (optional)

Preheat the oven to 160°C/320°F (fan-forced). Grease a 20 cm (8 in) springform cake tin and line the base with non-stick baking paper.

Make the almond pastry mixture. Press firmly into the base of the prepared tin and bake for 10–12 minutes or until just starting to brown around the edges. Set aside to cool and reduce the oven temperature to 130°C/265°F (fan-forced).

Put the dates in a small heatproof bowl and add 60 ml (2 fl oz/¼ cup) boiling water. Set aside for 5–10 minutes to cool, stirring occasionally. Whiz the soaked dates, including their soaking water, in a food processor until smooth. Add the ricotta, cream cheese, egg yolks, lemon zest and juice, and vanilla seeds and process until smooth. Sprinkle over the cornflour and whiz again until combined. Spoon the mixture into a large bowl. Beat the egg whites and salt with an electric mixer until soft peaks form. Gently fold into the cheese mixture in two batches.

Pour the mixture over the prepared base and bake for 30–35 minutes or until lightly browned and the centre is just set – it should wobble slightly. Turn off the oven and leave to cool with the door closed for 1 hour. Chill in the refrigerator for 3 hours or overnight. Remove from the tin. Just before serving, top the cheesecake with the figs or fruits of your choice, and drizzle with rice malt syrup if you like.

This cheesecake will keep for 2–3 days, covered, in the refrigerator.

I love the texture the ricotta gives this delicious cheesecake. The figs add little pops of sweetness and the chocolate and hazelnuts delightful crunch.

Ricotta, fig & hazelnut cheesecake

Serves 10–12

225 g (8 oz/1½ cups) plain (all-purpose) flour
100 g (3½ oz) cold butter, chopped
55 g (2 oz/½ cup) hazelnut meal
2 teaspoons baking powder
1 egg, lightly beaten
½ teaspoon liquid stevia
cream and fresh fruit, to serve (optional)

Filling
500 g (1 lb 2 oz) fresh firm ricotta cheese
100 ml (3½ fl oz) marsala
100 g (3½ oz) dark chocolate (70–85% cocoa solids), chopped
100 g (3½ oz) dried figs, chopped
70 g (2½ oz/½ cup) chopped hazelnuts

Grease a 23 cm (9 in) springform cake tin and line the base with non-stick baking paper.

Whiz the flour, butter, hazelnut meal, baking powder, egg and stevia in a food processor until the mixture resembles breadcrumbs. Press half of the mixture (reserving the remainder for the topping) into the base of the prepared tin and refrigerate until required.

Preheat the oven to 160°C/320°F (fan-forced).

For the filling, whiz the ricotta and marsala in a food processor until smooth. Transfer to a bowl and stir in the chocolate, fig and hazelnuts.

Pour the mixture over the prepared base and sprinkle over the remaining 'breadcrumbs'. Bake for 40–45 minutes, or until the top is lightly browned and the centre is just firm. Cool in the tin for 15 minutes. This cheesecake may be served warm or cold. Serve with fresh fruit and cream on the side if you like.

This cheesecake will keep for 2–3 days, covered, in the refrigerator.

This is my healthier cake version of the ubiquitous Oreo cookie. It makes a great dessert, but really, there's no need to save it for a special after-dinner occasion — I keep coming back for a sneaky slice every time I have a cup of tea. You will need to start this cake a few hours before you need it, as the macadamias are best soaked for a couple of hours to soften them slightly before blending for the vanilla cream.

Chocolaty sweet potato & macadamia cream cake

Serves 10–12
Gluten free

1 large orange sweet potato (about 420 g/15 oz), peeled and chopped
75 g (2¾ oz/½ cup) gluten-free plain (all-purpose) flour
50 g (1¾ oz/½ cup) cocoa powder (unsweetened)
1 teaspoon baking powder
½ teaspoon bicarbonate of soda (baking soda)
115 g (4 oz/⅓ cup) rice malt syrup
100 g (3½ oz) butter, melted
150 g (5½ oz/½ cup) Apple purée (page 162)

2 teaspoons natural vanilla extract
3 eggs
1 teaspoon apple cider vinegar
Dutch-processed cocoa powder, to dust

Macadamia vanilla cream
150 g (5½ oz/1 cup) macadamias
about 80 ml (2½ fl oz/⅓ cup) coconut milk
1 tablespoon rice malt syrup
1 tablespoon melted virgin coconut oil
3 teaspoons natural vanilla extract

To make the macadamia vanilla cream, soak the macadamias in cold water for about 2 hours, to soften slightly. Drain and rinse well. Put 60 ml (2 fl oz/¼ cup) coconut milk, the rice malt syrup, coconut oil, vanilla extract and finally the macadamias in a blender and blend until smooth, stopping occasionally to scrape down the sides of the blender, if required. Add a little more coconut milk if needed to keep the mixture moving — but not too much as the mixture should be quite thick and creamy. Transfer to a bowl and refrigerate until required.

Steam or microwave the sweet potato until tender. Drain, mash and set aside to cool. You will need 260 g (9 oz/1 cup) sweet potato for this cake.

Preheat the oven to 160°C/320°F (fan-forced). Grease a 20 cm (8 in) cake tin and line the base with non-stick baking paper.

Sift the flour, cocoa powder, baking powder and bicarbonate of soda into a bowl. In another bowl, whisk the rice malt syrup and butter until combined, then whisk in the sweet potato, apple purée and vanilla extract. Whisk the flour mixture in to the sweet potato mixture alternately with the eggs until combined.

Working quickly, stir the vinegar into the mixture and immediately spoon it into the prepared tin. Bake for 35–40 minutes or until just firm to the touch and a skewer inserted into the centre comes out clean. Remove from the oven and cool for 10 minutes before turning out onto a wire rack to cool completely.

Slice the cooled cake in half horizontally using a long serrated knife. Place the bottom layer on a serving plate or cake stand and spread with the macadamia vanilla cream. Top with the remaining cake half, dust with cocoa powder and serve.

This cake will keep for 2–3 days, covered, in the refrigerator.

Celebration Cakes

It's hard to beat a great carrot cake with lemony cream cheese frosting. The 'naked' method (where you don't add an outer layer of frosting) I've used here for icing the cake, is quick and easy, with spectacular results. Decorate the cake with edible flowers from the garden, if you have them.

Carrot cake with lemon cream-cheese frosting

Serves 16–20

350 g (12½ oz/2⅓ cups) plain (all-purpose) flour
1 tablespoon baking powder
1 tablespoon ground cinnamon
1 teaspoon ground nutmeg
½ teaspoon ground cloves
160 g (5½ oz/1 cup) dextrose
310 ml (10½ fl oz/1¼ cups) macadamia or sunflower oil
200 g (7 oz/⅔ cup) Apple purée (page 162)
6 eggs
3 carrots (about 350 g /12½ oz), finely grated
150 g (5½ oz/1½ cups) walnuts or pecans, roughly chopped (optional)
1 quantity Lemon cream-cheese frosting (page 166)
edible flowers, to decorate (optional)

Preheat the oven to 160°C/320°F (fan-forced). Grease three 4 cm (1½ in) deep, 20 cm (8 in) round cake tins and line the bases with non-stick baking paper. If you don't have three tins, you can cook the cakes in two batches.

Sift the flour, baking powder and spices into a large bowl and set aside.

Whisk the dextrose, oil, apple purée and eggs together in a large bowl until well combined. Stir in the carrot and nuts (if using), then fold in the sifted flour mixture.

Divide the cake batter evenly between the prepared tins (I like to weigh it – about 500 g (1 lb 2 oz) of batter for each tin). Smooth the surface with a spatula and bake for 18–20 minutes or until a skewer inserted into the centre comes out clean. Remove from the oven and leave to cool for 10 minutes before turning out onto a wire rack to cool completely.

Make the lemon cream-cheese frosting.

If the cakes are slightly domed, trim the tops off to level them with a long sharp serrated knife.

Put a little dollop of frosting in the centre of a serving plate and place four strips of baking paper around the edge. This will help to keep the plate clean of any icing. Place one layer of cake on the prepared plate. Spread about 160 g (5½ oz) of the frosting over the cake, taking it just over the edges. Repeat with the remaining two layers, placing the top layer of the cake bottom-side up (to achieve a sharp edge). Spread the remaining frosting over the top and side of the cake. Smooth off any excess frosting to achieve a 'naked' effect, just exposing the side of the cake. Remove the protective strips of baking paper from under the edges of the cake. Decorate with edible flowers, if desired.

This cake can be made a day in advance and stored in the refrigerator, covered loosely with plastic wrap. Decorate with flowers, just before serving.

This show-stopper can be prepared a day in advance although you may need to remove a shelf from your refrigerator to make enough room! Make the cake, layer, frost and drizzle with chocolate, then chill until about one hour before serving for the frosting to come back to room temperature. You can make the peanut brittle in advance (just make sure you store it in an airtight container), but don't add it to the cake until ready to serve.

Chocolate layer cake with peanut butter frosting

Serves 20–24

2 quantities Everyday chocolate cake (page 96), omitting the icing
1 quantity Peanut butter frosting (page 166)
2 tablespoons roasted black sesame seeds
handful freshly popped popcorn

Peanut brittle
240 g (8½ oz/1½ cups) dextrose
1 tablespoon glucose syrup

75 g (2¾ oz) butter, chopped
½ teaspoon bicarbonate of soda (baking soda)
150 g (5½ oz/1 cup) roasted salted peanuts

Chocolate drizzle
100 g (3½ oz) dark chocolate (70–85% cocoa solids), roughly chopped
100 g (3½ oz) butter, chopped
2 teaspoons glucose syrup

Make the chocolate cakes, omitting the icing. You will need four layers of cake for this recipe.

To make the peanut brittle, line two large baking trays with non-stick baking paper. Put the dextrose, glucose syrup and 80 ml (2½ fl oz/⅓ cup) water in a large saucepan over medium-high heat. Cook, gently swirling occasionally until the glucose has dissolved. Bring to the boil and cook, without stirring, until you have a golden caramel, about 10 minutes. Remove from the heat and add the butter gradually, whisking well between each addition, until combined. Stir in the bicarbonate of soda, taking care as the mixture will bubble up slightly. Working quickly, stir in the peanuts and pour the mixture over one of the prepared trays. Place another piece of baking paper on top and use a rolling pin to flatten the mixture as much as possible. When the caramel is cool enough to handle, after about 5 minutes, stretch sections of the mixture, starting from the edges, to create interesting shapes. Set aside to cool. Snap larger sections into shards. Any leftovers can be stored in an airtight container for up to a week.

Make the peanut butter frosting. If the cakes are domed, trim the tops off to level them with a serrated knife.

Put a little dollop of frosting in the centre of a serving plate and place four strips of baking paper around the edge. This will help to keep the plate clean of any icing. Place one layer of cake on the prepared plate. Spread about 80 g (2¾ oz/½ cup) of the frosting over the cake, taking it just over the edges. Repeat with the remaining three layers, placing the top layer of the cake bottom side up (to achieve a sharp edge). Spread a little more frosting thinly over the top and side of the cake. Scrape off any excess frosting and discard it (especially if it contains crumbs). This is called the 'crumb coat' and will keep the final layer of icing crumb-free. Put the cake in the refrigerator for the frosting to firm up, about 30 minutes.

For the final layer of icing, spread the top and side of the cake generously with the remaining frosting, smoothing the side with a long spatula. Using a gentle throwing action, throw pinches of the sesame seeds at the base of the cake. Most of it should stick! Put the cake back in the refrigerator for the icing to firm, about 30 minutes.

To make the chocolate drizzle, combine the chocolate, butter and glucose syrup in a heatproof bowl and melt over a saucepan of simmering water. Stir until combined. Remove from the heat and set aside to cool to almost room temperature. The mixture needs to be runny enough to pour, but not so warm that it will melt the frosting on the cake. Working quickly, pour the chocolate onto the top of the cake and use an offset spatula to spread it evenly over the top, allowing the mixture to drip down the sides. Just before serving, decorate the top of the cake with the shards of peanut brittle and the popcorn.

The undecorated cake can be made a day in advance and stored in the refrigerator. Once decorated, it is best eaten straight away. The cake is best served at room temperature; otherwise the frosting will be very firm.

Matcha green tea powder has a great flavour and colour. The cake pops add an
additional fun element!

Coconut matcha cake with matcha cake pops

Serves 16–20

2 quantities Coconut cake (page 97), omitting
   the syrup
1 tablespoon matcha green tea powder
roasted black sesame seeds, to decorate

Matcha cake pops
350 g (12½ oz) coconut cake trimmings
100 g (3½ oz) cream cheese, softened
40 g (1½ oz) butter, softened
1 tablespoon rice malt syrup
¼ teaspoon matcha green tea powder

200 g (7 oz) dark chocolate (70–85% cocoa solids),
   roughly chopped
1 tablespoon melted virgin coconut oil
15–20 lollipop sticks
2 tablespoons roasted black sesame seeds

Coconut Swiss meringue buttercream
½ quantity Swiss meringue buttercream
   (page 167), omitting the natural vanilla extract
2 tablespoons coconut cream
few drops natural coconut extract (optional)

Make the coconut cakes, adding 2 teaspoons of matcha to the flour mixture for each cake. Cool completely and trim the top of each cake with a long serrated knife. Set aside the trimmings for the cake pops. You will need about 350 g (12½ oz) of trimmings in total to make the cake pops.

For the cake pops, crumble the cake trimmings with your fingertips to resemble breadcrumbs. Beat the cream cheese, butter, rice malt syrup and matcha in a large bowl with an electric mixer until light and fluffy. Add the cake crumbs and stir until well combined. Roll tablespoonfuls of the mixture into balls and refrigerate for 1–2 hours or until firm.

Combine the chocolate and coconut oil in a heatproof bowl and melt over a saucepan of simmering water. Remove from the heat and leave to cool slightly.

Remove the cake pop balls from the refrigerator and insert a lollipop stick in to each ball. Dip about half of the cake balls fully in the chocolate to coat, allowing the excess chocolate to drip off, then sprinkle immediately with sesame seeds. Insert each cake pop stick into a foam block or place on a baking tray lined with baking paper. Refrigerate until set. For variation, half-dip some of the pops in the chocolate and leave some naked.

Make the Swiss meringue buttercream, omitting the vanilla extract. Add the coconut cream and coconut extract (if using) gradually, beating on low speed until combined.

Put a little dollop of frosting in the centre of a serving plate and place four strips of baking paper around the edge. This will help to keep the plate clean of any icing. Place one layer of cake on the prepared plate. Spread about 160 g (5½ oz/1 cup) of the buttercream over the cake, taking it just over the edges. Top with the second cake, placing it bottom-side up (to achieve a sharp edge). Spread the remaining buttercream over the top and side of the cake. Remove the protective strips of baking paper from under the edges of the cake and add the cake pops to the top of the cake. Decorate with a sprinkling of black sesame seeds.

This cake can be made a day in advance and stored in the refrigerator. Cover carefully with plastic wrap once the buttercream has set.

Roasted strawberries are really delicious. I especially love them with orange juice and rosewater.

Hazelnut, rose & orange cake with roasted strawberries & whipped ricotta

Serves 8–10
Gluten free

4 eggs
115 g (4 oz/⅓ cup) rice malt syrup
3 teaspoons rosewater
110 g (4 oz/¾ cup) gluten-free plain (all-purpose) flour
110 g (4 oz/1 cup) hazelnut meal
2 teaspoons baking powder
½ teaspoon xanthan gum
1 tablespoon finely grated orange zest
100 g (3½ oz) virgin coconut oil, melted
rose petals, to decorate (optional)

Roasted strawberries and whipped ricotta
500 g (1 lb 2 oz) strawberries, hulled and halved if large
juice of 1 orange
2 teaspoons rosewater, plus extra, to taste
500 g (1 lb 2 oz) fresh firm ricotta cheese
few drops of liquid stevia, to taste (optional)

Preheat the oven to 140°C/275°F (fan-forced). Lightly grease a deep 20 cm (8 in) cake tin and line the base with non-stick baking paper.

Beat the eggs, rice malt syrup and rose water in a large bowl with an electric mixer until thick and creamy, and the mixture leaves a thick trail when the beaters are lifted. Depending on your mixer, this may take about 10 minutes.

Sift the flour, hazelnut meal, baking powder and xanthan gum into a large bowl, returning any coarse hazelnut meal to the bowl with the flour. Gently fold the flour mixture into the egg mixture in two batches. Add the orange zest and melted coconut oil and fold through the mixture until just combined. Pour the mixture into the prepared tin, gently smooth the surface with a spatula and bake for 20–25 minutes, or until springy to touch in the centre and just starting to pull away from the side of the tin.

Remove from the oven and leave to cool for 5 minutes before turning out onto a wire rack to cool completely.

For the roasted strawberries and whipped ricotta, put the strawberries, orange juice and rosewater in a shallow roasting tin, cover loosely with foil and roast for 25–30 minutes, or until the strawberries are just starting to collapse. Remove from the oven and set aside to cool.

Whiz the ricotta in a food processor until smooth and silky. Add 8–10 strawberries and about 1 tablespoon of the syrup from the roasting pan. Taste the mixture and add a little more fruit, syrup, rosewater or liquid stevia to get a balanced flavour and a smooth, spreadable consistency. Cover and refrigerate until required.

Slice the cooled cake in half horizontally using a long serrated knife. Place the bottom layer on a serving plate or cake stand and spread over about half of the whipped ricotta. Top with the remaining cake, whipped ricotta, roasted strawberries and a drizzle of the syrup. Decorate with rose petals for extra prettiness, if desired.

I've made a chocolate patisserie cream for this impressive croquembouche, but you can use several of the fillings featured in this book — try mixing it up for delicious surprises! The Choc avocado mousse (page 76), Banana cashew cream (page 33) and Passionfruit cashew cream (page 28), or indeed a combination of these, are ideal.

Croquembouche

Makes 80–90 puffs

4 quantities Choux puff mixture (page 76)
35 cm (13¾ in) polystyrene cone (optional)
edible flowers, to decorate

Chocolate crème pâtissière
2 litres (68 fl oz) full-cream (whole) milk
1 tablespoon natural vanilla extract
300 g (10½ oz) dark chocolate (70–85% cocoa solids), chopped

320 g (11½ oz/2 cups) dextrose
4 eggs plus 8 egg yolks
200 g (7 oz/1⅓ cups) cornflour (cornstarch)
70 g (2½ oz/½ cup) Dutch-processed cocoa powder, sifted
80 ml (2¾ fl oz/⅓ cup) coffee liqueur (optional)

Toffee
800 g (1 lb 12 oz/5 cups) dextrose

To make the chocolate crème pâtissière, combine the milk and vanilla extract in a large heavy-based saucepan over medium heat and bring just to the boil. Remove from the heat and stir in the chopped chocolate until melted. Meanwhile, beat the dextrose, eggs and egg yolk in a large heatproof bowl with an electric mixer until thick and pale. Beat in the cornflour and cocoa. While still whisking, slowly pour the hot milk into the egg mixture and whisk until combined. Return the mixture to the cleaned saucepan and cook, whisking constantly by hand until the mixture thickens and just comes to the boil. Transfer the mixture to a large heatproof bowl, whisk to knock some of the heat out and set aside to cool. Press a piece of plastic wrap over the surface of the crème to stop a skin forming as it is cooling. Remove the plastic and whisk the crème every so often, to speed up the cooling process. Stir in the liqueur, if using, and put the mixture in a large piping bag fitted with a 5 mm (¼ in) plain nozzle. Chill in the refrigerator until completely cool. This crème pâtissière can also be made up to 2 days in advance.

Make the choux puff mixture in two batches. Put the dough in a piping bag fitted with a 1.5 cm (½ in) plain nozzle and pipe small dollops, about 3 cm x 3 cm (1¼ in x 1¼ in), onto the prepared trays about 4 cm (1½ in) apart. Pat any peaks down gently with a damp fingertip. Bake as directed, but instead of cutting the puffs in half, make a small hole in the base of each puff with a small sharp knife to release the steam. Bake for a second time to dry out, if necessary. Transfer to a wire rack and leave to cool.

When ready to assemble the croquembouche, insert the piping bag nozzle into the small hole in each puff and fill with crème pâtissière. You'll know when the puff is full, as it will feel heavy in your hand. Set aside on a baking tray.

For the toffee, it is easiest to work in two batches. Combine half of the dextrose and 125 ml (4 fl oz/½ cup) water in a large heavy-based saucepan over medium-high heat. Cook, stirring, until the dextrose is melted. Bring to the boil, without stirring. Brush down the side of the pan with a clean pastry brush dipped in water to remove any crystals that may form, if necessary. Cook to a light golden brown, about 10 minutes. Remove from the heat.

Very carefully dip the top of each filled puff in the toffee and place them toffee-side up on a baking tray lined with baking paper. Return the pan to the heat and warm it gently if the toffee is starting to set.

To assemble the croquembouche, starting with the largest of the puffs and working your way through to the smallest, dip their bases in toffee one by one and place 10–12 of them in a ring on a serving plate (or around the base of a cone, if using), sticking them together with the toffee. Drizzle the layer with a little extra toffee and continue to build up the layers to a peak at the top. Enlisting the help of a friend would be useful here!

When required, make the second batch of toffee with the remaining dextrose and 125 ml (4 fl oz/½ cup) water. Dot edible flowers around the croquembouche and drizzle or carefully flick any remaining toffee over and around your creation. Serve straight away.

This banana cream cheese frosting is sublime! The pineapple flowers take some time to dry out, but they don't require much effort. I've found that I get the best results with a ripe pineapple — the flowers have a better, brighter colour and dehydrate more rapidly. They're not only pretty, but edible and truly delicious, too. The pineapple flowers can be made a few days in advance.

Hummingbird layer cake with pineapple flowers

Serves 16–20

1 ripe pineapple
2 quantities Hummingbird cake (page 95), omitting the flaked coconut topping
citrus leaves, to decorate

Banana cream cheese frosting
2 quantities Lemon cream-cheese frosting (page 166), keeping the lemon juice separate
1 small banana, peeled

Preheat the oven to 80°C/175°F (fan-forced). Line two large baking trays with non-stick baking paper.

Top and tail the pineapple and cut away the skin. There will be some pineapple 'eyes' remaining, but don't worry, you can trim them later. Cut the pineapple into discs with a very sharp knife, about 2 mm (⅛ in) thick. Trim any remaining 'eyes', if necessary, and blot the pineapple discs on kitchen paper to soak up the excess moisture.

Place the discs on the prepared trays in a single layer and bake for 2–2½ hours, turning every half an hour, until the discs are almost dry and the edges are starting to turn up. Lightly press the discs into mini-muffin or cupcake tins to create flower-like shapes. Bake for a further 30 minutes or until the flowers hold their shapes when lifted. Leave to cool in the tins. If not using straight away, store in an airtight container for 3–4 days.

Make the hummingbird cakes, omitting the flaked coconut topping. Cool completely and cut one-third off the length of each cake. You will end up with two 20 cm (8 in) (approximately) squares and two rectangles to create three layers.

To make the banana cream cheese frosting, mash the banana in a bowl with a fork until quite smooth. You will need about 95 g (3¼ oz) mashed banana. Stir in the lemon juice from the lemon cream-cheese frosting recipe and set aside. Make the lemon cream-cheese frosting, then beat in the banana mixture at the same time as the dextrose. Spoon about 160 g (5½ oz/1 cup) of the frosting into a piping bag with a 1.5 cm (½ in) plain nozzle. Refrigerate until required.

Put a little dollop of frosting in the centre of a serving plate and place four strips of baking paper around the edge. This will help to keep the plate clean of any icing. Place one of the square cakes on the prepared plate. Spread about 160 g (5½ oz) of the frosting over the cake, taking it just over the edges. Repeat with the two rectangles, then the final square of cake, which you should place bottom-side up (to achieve sharp edges). Spread the remaining frosting over the top and sides of the cake. Remove the protective strips of baking paper from under the edges of the cake. Pipe little dollops of reserved frosting on the cake and decorate with the pineapple flowers and citrus leaves.

The cake can be stored in the refrigerator for up to 2 days, but is best served at room temperature or only slightly chilled.

I based this cake on the one I made for our wedding cake, over a decade ago. As soon as I tasted that hint of orange blossom and the texture I love from the semolina, I was instantly transported back in time to that happy and fun day.

Orange blossom, yoghurt & semolina cake

Serves 25–30

450 g (1 lb/2½ cups) fine semolina
225 g (8 oz/1½ cups) plain (all purpose) flour
120 g (4½ oz/1 cup) almond meal
1½ tablespoons baking powder
500 g (1 lb 2 oz) butter, softened
230 g (8 oz/⅔ cup) rice malt syrup
1 tablespoon finely grated orange zest
8 eggs, lightly beaten

2 teaspoons orange blossom water
1 teaspoon liquid stevia
500 g (1 lb 2 oz/2 cups) natural yoghurt
250 ml (8½ fl oz/1 cup) buttermilk
1 quantity Swiss meringue buttercream (page 167)
1 teaspoon beetroot (beet) juice (see page 137) or a few drops of natural pink food colouring
orange blossoms or other edible flowers and citrus leaves, to decorate

Preheat the oven to 160°C/320°F (fan-forced). Grease a 6 cm (2½ in) deep, 23 cm (9 in) round cake tin and a 7 cm (2¾ in) deep, 18 cm (7 in) round cake tin. Line the bases and sides with three layers of baking paper, extending the paper about 5 cm (2 in) above the edges of the tins.

Sift the semolina, flour, almond meal and baking powder into a large bowl. Beat the butter, rice malt syrup and orange zest with an electric mixer until light and fluffy. Gradually add the eggs. Fold in the orange blossom water and stevia, and then add the combined dry ingredients alternately with the yoghurt and finally the buttermilk.

Divide the cake mixture between the two prepared tins so that it reaches the same height in each tin. Smooth the surface with a spatula and bake for 45–50 minutes or until a skewer inserted into the centre comes out clean. Remove from the oven and leave to cool for 10 minutes before turning out onto a wire rack to cool completely.

Make the buttercream. Transfer about 160g (5½ oz/1 cup) of the buttercream to a separate bowl. Gently stir in enough beetroot juice to get a pretty pink colour to add a 'watercolour' effect to the cake. If the cakes are slightly domed, trim the tops off to level them with a long sharp serrated knife. Cut each cake in half horizontally.

Put a little dollop of frosting in the centre of a serving plate and place four strips of baking paper around the edge. This will help to keep the plate clean of any icing. Place one of the large cake layers on top and spread about 160 g (5½ oz/1 cup) of the plain buttercream over the cake, taking it just over the edge. Top with the remaining large cake layer and spread another cup of buttercream over the top and side of the cake. Scrape off any excess icing and discard it (especially if it contains crumbs). This is called the 'crumb coat' and will help to keep the final layer of icing crumb-free. Put the cake in the refrigerator for the icing to firm up, about 30 minutes. Repeat the process with the small cake layers, working on a baking paper-lined plate.

For the final layer of icing, using about half of the pink buttercream, dollop random patches over the sides and top of the large cake. Fill in the gaps with a generous amount of the plain buttercream and starting with the top, spread the top and side of the cake with the icing. You should have patches of pink here and there. Do not overwork the icing or it will all blend together. Repeat with the smaller cake and then place it off-centre, on top of the large cake.

Put any remaining pink buttercream and plain buttercream in a piping bag with a 1.5 cm (½ in) plain nozzle. Pipe little dollops of buttercream on the cake. Decorate with the edible flowers and leaves.

The cake can be stored in the refrigerator for several hours, but it is best served at room temperature; otherwise the buttercream icing will be very firm.

This spectacular cake is coloured with homemade natural food colouring.
Its innocent exterior belies the excitement when it is cut open!

Rainbow cake

Serves 16–20

675 g (1½ lb/4½ cups) plain flour
2 tablespoons baking powder
½ teaspoon bicarbonate of soda (baking soda)
180 ml (6 fl oz/¾ cup) full cream (whole) milk
2 tablespoons natural vanilla extract
1 teaspoon liquid stevia
375 g (13 oz) butter, softened
170 g (6 oz/½ cup) rice malt syrup
225 g (8 oz/¾ cup) Apple purée (page 162)

6 eggs
60 g (2 oz) shredded coconut
1 quantity Swiss meringue buttercream (page 167)

Natural food colours
80 g (2¾ oz/2 cups) baby spinach
1 beetroot (beet) (about 175 g/6 oz), peeled and
   roughly chopped
75 g (2¾ oz/½ cup) frozen blackberries, thawed
1 carrot (about 120 g/4½ oz), peeled and chopped

For the food colours, blend (I use a hand-held blender) the vegetables and fruit individually until puréed. Strain through a piece of muslin (cheesecloth), squeezing out as much juice as possible. You will need about 1 tablespoon spinach juice, 2 tablespoons beetroot juice for two pink cakes (one darker than the other), 5 teaspoons blackberry juice and 2½ tablespoons carrot juice, plus about 1 teaspoon of each juice per 2 tablespoons shredded coconut.

Preheat the oven to 160°C/320°F (fan-forced). Grease five 4 cm (1½ in) deep, 20 cm (8 in) round cake tins and line the bases with non-stick baking paper. If you don't have five tins, you can cook the cakes in batches.

Sift the flour, baking powder and bicarbonate of soda into a large bowl and combine. Combine the milk, vanilla extract and stevia in a jug. Beat the butter and rice malt syrup with an electric mixer until light and fluffy. Gradually add the egg, beating well between each addition. Add a spoonful or two of the flour mixture, if it seems like it is splitting. Beat in the apple purée. Fold in the remaining dry ingredients alternately with the milk mixture.

Divide the cake batter evenly between five separate bowls (I weigh it – about 400 g/14 oz per cake). Stir a different colouring into each bowl, adding a little more colouring if you would like a darker shade. Spoon into the prepared tins, smooth the surface with a spatula and bake for 15–18 minutes, or until a skewer inserted into the centre comes out clean. Remove from the oven and leave to cool for 5 minutes before turning out onto wire racks to cool.

Turn the oven down to 50°C/120°F (fan-forced). Divide 2 tablespoons of coconut between five small bowls and stir about 2 teaspoons of colouring into each. Keeping the colours separate, spread the coconut on baking trays lined with baking paper and bake for 20–30 minutes, stirring often until completely dry. Set aside to cool.

Make the Swiss meringue buttercream. If the cakes are slightly domed, trim the tops off to level them with a knife.

Put a little dollop of buttercream in the centre of a serving plate and place four strips of baking paper around the edge. This will help to keep the plate clean of any icing. Place one layer of cake on the prepared plate. Spread about 120 g (4½ oz/¾ cup) of the buttercream over the top, taking it just over the edge. Repeat with the remaining layers, placing the top layer bottom-side up (to achieve a sharp edge). Spread more buttercream thinly over the top and side of the cake. Scrape off any excess buttercream and discard it. This is called the 'crumb coat' and will help to keep you final layer of icing crumb-free. Put the cake in the refrigerator for the icing to firm up, about 30 minutes.

For the final layer of icing, spread the top and side of the cake generously with the remaining buttercream. Sprinkle with the coloured shredded coconut to decorate. The cake can be stored in the refrigerator for several hours before serving, but it is best served at room temperature; otherwise the buttercream icing will be very firm.

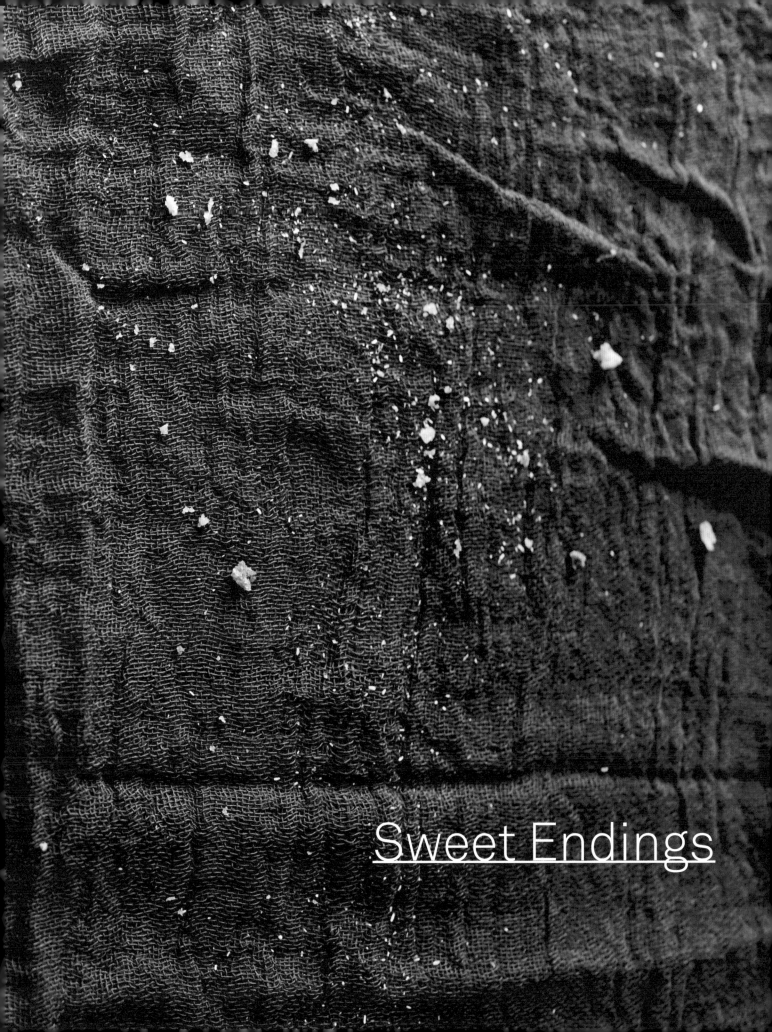

Sweet Endings

The simple yet delicious filling for this pie is fabulous served with just a dollop of cream or yoghurt (even for breakfast) — yet the impressive lattice top takes it to the next level. It takes a bit of patience but is worth the effort. I don't bother with peeling the apples — you may as well get the extra fibre from the skin, I say.

Rhubarb & apple pie

Serves 6–8
Can be made gluten free

½ quantity Rough puff pastry (page 164) or Gluten-free rough puff pastry (page 165)
30 g (1 oz) butter
3 large apples (about 600 g/1 lb 5 oz), cored and thinly sliced
450 g (1 lb) rhubarb, cut into 2.5 cm (1 in) pieces
finely grated zest and juice of 1 orange
2 tablespoons rice malt syrup
2 tablespoons cornflour (cornstarch)
1 teaspoon mixed spice
1 egg, lightly beaten
cream, crème fraîche or creamy yoghurt, to serve

Roll out the pastry on a lightly floured surface to about 3 mm (⅛ in) thick. Cut a 1.5 cm (½ in) strip of pastry from the edge and press it around the rim of a 24 cm (9½ in) pie dish. Rub the rim of the dish with a little softened butter to help the pastry stick if necessary. This will create a nice finished edge on the pie when you add the lattice. Set aside in the refrigerator. Cut the remaining pastry into strips 4 cm (1½ in) wide. You will need at least eight strips. Place on a baking paper-lined tray and refrigerate until required.

Melt the butter in a large saucepan over medium–low heat. Add the apples, rhubarb, orange zest and juice, and rice malt syrup and cook for 5–6 minutes, or until the fruits are just starting to soften. Remove from the heat and stir in the cornflour and mixed spice. Transfer to the pie dish and set aside to cool.

Preheat the oven to 180°C/350°F (fan-forced).

Brush the pastry on the rim of the pie dish with a little water and arrange the pastry strips in a lattice pattern over the filling, pressing the strips onto the pastry rim to seal. Trim excess pastry. Brush lightly with the beaten egg, trying not to let it dribble down the sides of the pastry strips.

Bake for 20 minutes or until the pastry is starting to puff and is lightly coloured. Reduce the oven temperature to 160°C/320°F (fan-forced) and cook for another 20–25 minutes or until the pastry is golden and the filling is bubbling.

Remove from the oven and allow to settle for 10 minutes before serving with cream, crème fraîche or yoghurt.

If you have a tree overflowing with lemons, this recipe is a great
way to use them up. You will need about four lemons for this recipe. I
love the tartness and the silky texture of this lemony tart, and the crust
is a versatile gluten-free beauty. Try it with the pumpkin pie as well.

Lemon tart

Serves 10–12
Gluten free

1 tablespoon finely grated lemon zest
160 ml (5½ fl oz/⅔ cup) freshly squeezed lemon juice
85 g (3 oz/¼ cup) rice malt syrup
180 g (6½ oz/¾ cup) mascarpone
4 eggs, plus 1 egg extra, lightly beaten, to brush
cream, crème fraîche or creamy yoghurt, to serve (optional)

Almond pastry crust
240 g (8½ oz/2 cups) almond meal
2 tablespoons coconut flour
60 g (2 oz) virgin coconut oil, chilled to solidify then roughly chopped
1 egg
½ teaspoon liquid stevia (optional)
2–4 teaspoons iced water

Preheat the oven to 160°C/320°F (fan-forced).

For the almond pastry crust, whiz the almond meal, coconut flour and solid coconut oil in a food processor
and pulse until the coconut oil is mixed evenly throughout the mixture – you will still see small flecks of the
solid coconut oil. Add the egg and stevia (if using), and, with the processor running, add enough water for
the mixture to form coarse crumbs. It should cling together when pressed between your fingertips.

Distribute the crumbs evenly over the base and up the side of a fluted 23 cm x 3 cm (9 in x 1¼ in) round
loose-based tart tin, and then press the mixture firmly into the base and side of the tin with your fingertips.

Cover the crust with a sheet of non-stick baking paper and fill with baking weights, or dry rice or beans.
Blind bake for 10 minutes, remove from the oven and take out the weights and paper. Brush with the extra
beaten egg and bake for a further 10 minutes or until the crust is cooked through and the sides are lightly
coloured. Remove from the oven and set aside to cool.

Whisk the lemon zest and juice, and the rice malt syrup together until the syrup dissolves. Add the
mascarpone and eggs, and whisk gently until combined. Try not to whisk too vigorously or you will end
up with little bubbles sitting on top of the cooked tart.

Put the cooled crust on a baking tray and place on the oven shelf. Pour the lemon mixture carefully into the
crust. Bake for 25–30 minutes or until set with a slight wobble in the centre. Remove from the oven and cool
in the tin. Serve at room temperature or chilled with cream, crème fraîche or yoghurt, if desired.

Roasting the pumpkin intensifies its sweetness and the caramelised edges of the pumpkin add a lovely complexity to this pumpkin pie filling. The filo pastry gives a crisp but light crust. To make this gluten free try the almond crust recipe from the Lemon tart on page 143.

Roasted pumpkin pie

Serves 8–10
Can be made gluten free

500 g (1 lb 2 oz) peeled butternut pumpkin (squash), cut into 2 cm (¾ in) pieces
8 sheets filo pastry
40 g (1½ oz) butter, melted
100 g (3½ oz/⅓ cup) Apple purée (page 162)
3 eggs
1 teaspoon ground cinnamon
1 teaspoon ground nutmeg
½ teaspoon liquid stevia
300 ml (10 fl oz) thickened (double/heavy) cream
2 tablespoons pepitas (pumpkin seeds)
whipped cream or yoghurt, to serve

Preheat the oven to 180°C/350°F (fan-forced). Line a baking tray with non-stick baking paper.

Scatter the pumpkin in a single layer on the prepared tray. Roast for 30–35 minutes until tender. Set aside to cool.

Reduce the oven temperature to 160°C/320°F (fan-forced). Grease a fluted 23 cm x 3 cm (9 in x 1¼ in) round loose-based tart tin.

On a work surface, layer the filo, placing the second sheet at 90 degrees over the first, creating a criss-cross shape, and brushing each sheet of pastry with the melted butter. Continue with the remaining sheets, rotating the angle so that you end up with a complete circle of layered pastry, large enough to fit the tin. Lift into the tin, press gently to fit, then trim with a pair of kitchen scissors, leaving the edge slightly overhanging.

Cover the pastry with a sheet of baking paper and fill with baking weights, or dry rice or beans. Blind bake for 10 minutes, remove the weights and paper, and bake for a further 10 minutes or until the base is cooked through and the sides are lightly coloured. Remove from the oven and set aside to cool.

Whiz the cooled pumpkin, apple purée, eggs, spices, stevia and cream in a food processor until smooth.

Pour into the pie case and sprinkle the pepitas over the top. Bake for 55–60 minutes or until browned and set in the centre. Cool and serve with whipped cream or yoghurt.

You can blanch and peel your fruit if you like, but I don't think it's necessary for this recipe. Try other stone fruit in season – apricots, plums and cherries would all work really well.

Peach, nectarine & ginger crumble

Serves 6–8
Gluten free

3 peaches (about 600 g/1 lb 5 oz)
3 nectarines (about 600 g/1 lb 5 oz)
1 tablespoon cornflour (cornstarch)
1 teaspoon finely grated fresh ginger
finely grated zest and juice of 1 orange
cream, crème fraîche or thick yoghurt, to serve

Crumble topping
70 g (2½ oz/⅔ cup) quinoa flakes
60 g (2 oz/½ cup) pecans, chopped roughly
25 g (1 oz/½ cup) flaked coconut
10 g (¼ oz/⅓ cup) puffed wholegrain rice
1 teaspoon ground ginger
80 g (2¾ oz) butter or virgin coconut oil, melted
2 tablespoons rice malt syrup

Preheat the oven to 160°C/320°F (fan-forced).

Halve the peaches and nectarines, remove the stones and cut into wedges. Toss with the cornflour and ginger in a large bowl, and then with the orange zest and juice. Pile into a 1 litre (34 fl oz) baking dish or four 250 ml (8½ fl oz/1 cup) ramekins.

For the crumble topping, combine the quinoa flakes, pecans, coconut, puffed rice and ginger in a large bowl. Drizzle with the melted butter or oil and the rice malt syrup. Stir until well combined.

Sprinkle the crumble mixture over the fruit. Bake for 35–40 minutes or until the fruit is bubbling and the top is golden and crisp. Cover with foil if the top is browning too quickly. Serve with a dollop of cream, crème fraîche or thick yoghurt.

Left to right
**Roasted pumpkin pie;
Peach, nectarine &
ginger crumble**

You could use only apples for this recipe, but why not mix it up? Just about any apple or pear will work well for this dish. The Middle Eastern flavours are utterly delicious.

Orange blossom-baked apples & pears

Serves 6
Gluten free

3 large apples (about 600 g/1 lb 5 oz), cored
3 pears (about 600 g/1 lb 5 oz), cored
100 g (3½ oz) fresh (medjool) dates, pitted and chopped roughly
40 g (1½ oz/¼ cup) almonds, chopped roughly
35 g (1¼ oz/¼ cup) roughly chopped dried apricots
finely grated zest and juice of 2 oranges
1 tablespoon orange blossom water
30 g (1 oz) butter, softened
Labne (see page 153), creamy yoghurt or mascarpone, to serve

Preheat the oven to 160°C/320°F (fan-forced).

Use a small sharp knife to score a spiral around each piece of fresh fruit, cutting just through the skin.

Combine the dates, almonds, apricots, zest and 2 teaspoons of the orange blossom water in a bowl. Divide between the cored fruit, pushing it firmly into the cavity and put in a 1 litre (34 fl oz) baking dish. Sprinkle over the remaining orange blossom water and orange juice, and scatter with dots of butter.

Cover the dish with foil and bake for 30 minutes or until the whole fruit is just soft. Remove the foil and bake for a further 15–20 minutes or until tender.

Serve with labne, yoghurt or mascarpone.

Tarte Tatin is a classic dessert and just as delicious made with rice malt syrup. It really is a worthwhile exercise making your own pastry — rough puff is the cheat's version of puff, and so not quite as tricky to make. Don't throw your pastry scraps away, cut them into pieces, bake and enjoy the crunchy morsels later on.

Tarte Tatin

Serves 8–10

6 granny smith apples (about 1 kg/2 lb 3 oz), peeled, cored and quartered
2 tablespoons lemon juice
½ teaspoon ground cinnamon
170 g (6 oz/½ cup) rice malt syrup
40 g (1½ oz) butter, sliced thinly
½ quantity Rough puff pastry (page 164)
cream, crème fraîche or creamy yoghurt, to serve

Toss the apples with the lemon juice and cinnamon in a large bowl.

Drizzle the rice malt syrup over the base of a 20 cm (8 in) heavy-based ovenproof frying pan or tarte tatin pan and scatter with the butter. Add the apple quarters, cut-side up, tightly packing them in a single layer.

Cook the apples over medium heat for 10–15 minutes or until the syrup is beginning to caramelise and the apples are just tender. There will be quite a bit of juice in the pan. Remove from the heat and set aside to cool for about 30 minutes.

Meanwhile, preheat the oven to 180°C/350°F (fan-forced).

Roll out the pastry on a lightly floured surface to about 3 mm (⅛ in) thick and cut a circle slightly larger than the pan. Prick the pastry all over with a fork and place it on top of the apples. Ease the pastry down between the apples and the side of the pan.

Bake for 25–30 minutes or until the pastry is cooked through, puffed and a deep golden brown. You should see the juices bubbling up the sides. Remove from the oven and allow to settle for 10 minutes.

Place a large serving plate upside-down on top of the pan and carefully turn the tart upside down onto the plate. Serve warm or cold with cream, crème fraîche or yoghurt.

I love the combination of roasted rhubarb with the sweetness of strawberries. This dessert is finished off beautifully with the crispy topping. The crumble mixture even makes great biscuits if you roll it into balls, flatten slightly onto a tray and bake for about 15 minutes. Only add the rice malt syrup if you think the fruit is not at its peak, to balance out any tartness.

Rhubarb & strawberry crispy crumble

Serves 6–8
Wheat free

450 g (1 lb) trimmed rhubarb, cut into 3 cm (1¼ in) pieces
500 g (1 lb 2 oz) strawberries, hulled and halved if large
2 teaspoons vanilla bean paste
1 tablespoon rice malt syrup (optional)
finely grated zest and juice of 1 large orange
cream, crème fraîche or thick yoghurt, to serve

Crispy crumble topping
135 g (5 oz/1¼ cups) rolled (porridge) oats
50 g (1¾ oz/⅓ cup) gluten-free plain (all-purpose) flour
1 teaspoon ground cinnamon
80 g (2¾ oz) chilled butter, chopped
2 tablespoons rice malt syrup
40 g (1½ oz/½ cup) flaked almonds

Preheat the oven to 160°C/320°F (fan-forced).

In a large bowl, combine the rhubarb, strawberries, vanilla, rice malt syrup (if using) and the orange zest and juice. Pile into a 1 litre (34 fl oz) baking dish or four 250 ml (8½ fl oz/1 cup) ramekins.

For the crumble topping, combine the oats, flour and cinnamon in a large bowl. Add the butter and drizzle with the rice malt syrup. Use your fingertips to rub in the butter and syrup until well combined. Stir in the almonds.

Sprinkle the crumble mixture over the top of the fruit, leaving little clumps of different sizes. Bake for 35–40 minutes or until the fruit is bubbling and the top is golden and crisp. Cover with foil if the top is browning too quickly. Serve with a dollop of cream, crème fraîche or thick yoghurt.

This tart is perfect for when you need something light and lovely to finish a meal. Prepare the labne the night before for a luscious, thick texture. Make sure you buy pot-set yoghurt, rather than stirred or creamy yoghurt – it will strain more easily.

Creamy raspberry & orange tart

Serves 6
Gluten free

120 g (4½ oz/½ cup) mascarpone
about 1½ tablespoons orange liqueur or freshly squeezed orange juice
125 g (4½ oz) fresh raspberries
rice malt syrup, to serve (optional)

Labne
250 g (9 oz/1 cup) natural pot-set yoghurt
1 teaspoon finely grated orange zest

Almond pastry crust
120 g (4½ oz/1 cup) almond meal
1 tablespoon coconut flour
30 g (1 oz) virgin coconut oil, chilled and roughly chopped
1 egg white
3–4 drops liquid stevia (optional)

To make the labne, combine the yoghurt and zest and place in a fine-meshed sieve lined with muslin. Place over a bowl, then cover and pop in the refrigerator for 12–24 hours to drain and thicken. This makes a little more labne than is needed for this recipe – save any leftovers to dollop on your breakfast cereal.

For the almond pastry crust, preheat the oven to 160°C/320°F (fan-forced). Whiz the almond meal, coconut flour and solid coconut oil in a food processor until the coconut oil is mixed evenly throughout the mixture – you will still see small flecks of the solid coconut oil. Add the egg white and stevia (if using) and pulse until the mixture forms coarse crumbs. It should cling together when pressed between your fingertips.

Distribute the crumbs evenly over the base and up the side of a fluted 20 cm x 3 cm (8 in x 1¼ in) round loose-based tart tin, and then press the mixture firmly into the base and side of the tin with your fingertips. The layer will seem very thin, but don't worry, it will hold together very well.

Cover the crust with a sheet of non-stick baking paper and fill with baking weights, or dry rice or beans. Blind bake for 10 minutes, remove the weights and paper, and bake for a further 10 minutes or until the crust is cooked through and the sides are lightly coloured. Remove from the oven and set aside to cool.

Mix 130 g (4½ oz/½ cup) of the labne with the mascarpone and 1 tablespoon of the liqueur or orange juice together until combined. Taste and add a little more liqueur or juice to adjust the flavour and consistency if you like. Spread into the cooled crust.

Toss the raspberries with the remaining liqueur or orange juice and scatter over the top of the tart. Drizzle with a little rice malt syrup if desired.

Left to right
Rhubarb & strawberry crispy crumble; Creamy raspberry & orange tart

Pandan extract is available from Asian grocery stores. The strength can vary between brands, so add it gradually. You can prepare the crèmes the day before serving — they need to be well chilled before you brûlée the top. You will need a kitchen blow torch for this task. Don't be tempted to add too much syrup to the top of each crème — it will take too long to caramelise.

Coconut & pandan crème brûlée

Serves 6
Gluten free

400 ml (13½ fl oz) tin coconut milk
250 ml (8½ fl oz/1 cup) thickened (double/heavy) cream
½–1 teaspoon pandan extract
2 eggs plus 4 egg yolks
2 tablespoons rice malt syrup, plus extra to drizzle
tropical fruit, to serve (optional)

Preheat the oven to 150°C/300°F (fan-forced). Fold a clean dish towel into the base a large, deep baking dish and place six 125 ml (4 fl oz/½ cup) capacity ramekins on top of the towel.

Heat the coconut milk, cream and pandan extract in a saucepan over medium–low heat. Cook, stirring occasionally until the mixture almost comes to the boil, about 10 minutes.

Meanwhile, gently whisk the egg, egg yolks and rice malt syrup in a large heatproof bowl until well combined. Gradually whisk in the coconut mixture and then strain into a large heatproof jug. Stand for 5 minutes and, using a large spoon, remove and discard any foam from the top of the mixture.

Divide the coconut mixture evenly between the ramekins. Place the baking dish on the shelf of the oven and carefully add enough boiling water to come halfway up the sides of the ramekins, ensuring that the dish towel is completely submerged. (This is easier than trying to transport a dish full of water from the bench to the oven).

Bake for 20–25 minutes or until set with a slight wobble in the centre. Cool for 30 minutes and then refrigerate for at least 3 hours until firm.

Working one at a time, drizzle about 1 teaspoon of rice malt syrup over the surface of each crème. Caramelise the syrup carefully with a kitchen blow torch, swirling the syrup over the surface as you go. Set aside to cool and harden, and then repeat with the remaining brûlées. Serve with tropical fruit, if desired.

To make this aromatic pudding extra special, you can 'brûlée' the top. Just follow the instructions for the Coconut and pandan crème brûlée on page 156.

Baked kaffir lime & coconut rice pudding

Serves 4–6
Gluten free

65 g (2¼ oz/⅓ cup) medium grain rice
4 kaffir lime leaves, bruised, plus extra, finely shredded to serve
1 stalk lemongrass, cut into sections, split and bruised
1 vanilla bean, split and seeds scraped
1 tablespoon rice malt syrup (optional)
600 ml (20½ fl oz) full cream (whole) milk
400 ml (13½ fl oz) tin coconut milk
½ teaspoon liquid stevia (optional)
lime segments, to serve

Preheat the oven to 160°C/320°F (fan-forced).

Combine the rice, bruised lime leaves, lemongrass, vanilla bean and seeds, rice malt syrup (if using) and the milks in a saucepan over medium heat. Cook, stirring occasionally, for 8–10 minutes or until the mixture just comes to a simmer. Remove from the heat and set aside for 20 minutes for the flavours to infuse.

Remove and discard the lime leaves, lemongrass and the vanilla bean. Pour the mixture into a 1 litre (34 fl oz) ovenproof dish (or four 250 ml (8½ fl oz/1 cup) capacity ramekins). Bake, stirring occasionally, for 1 hour 15 minutes – 1 hour 30 minutes for the large dish, and 1 hour – 1 hour 10 minutes for the ramekins, or until the rice is tender and the mixture is very creamy. When a skin begins to form, try to stir underneath the skin if you can. Stir less frequently towards the end of the cooking time.

Remove from the oven and set aside for 10 minutes to rest before serving. Sprinkle with shredded lime leaves and segments. The pudding may also be served cold.

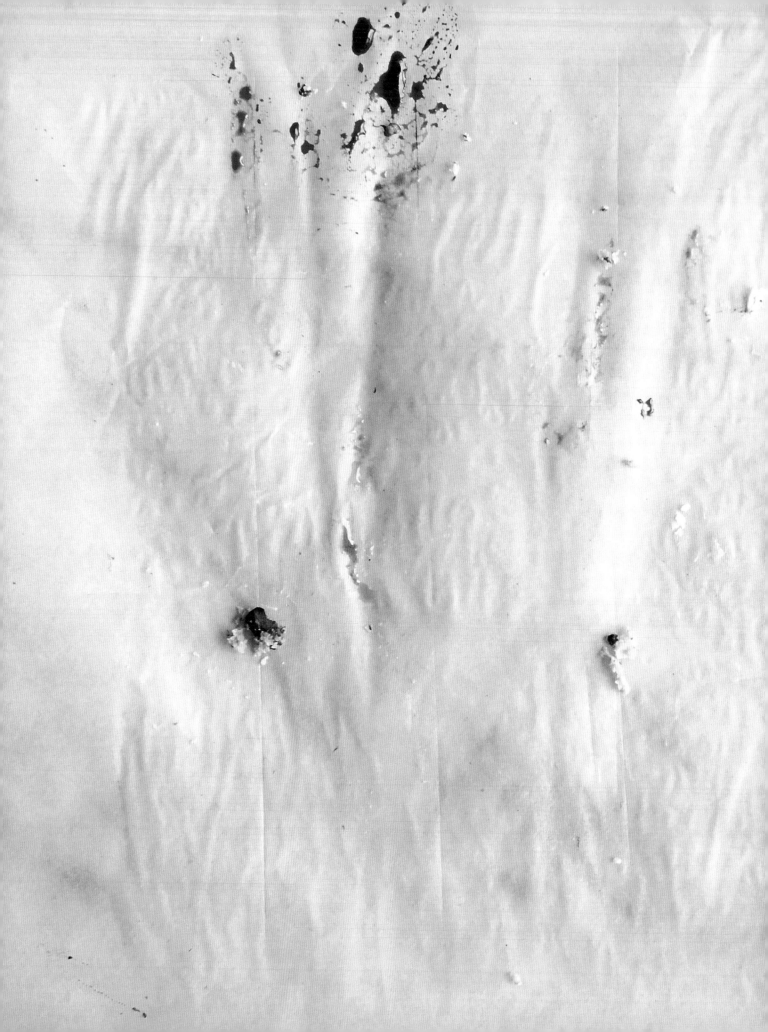

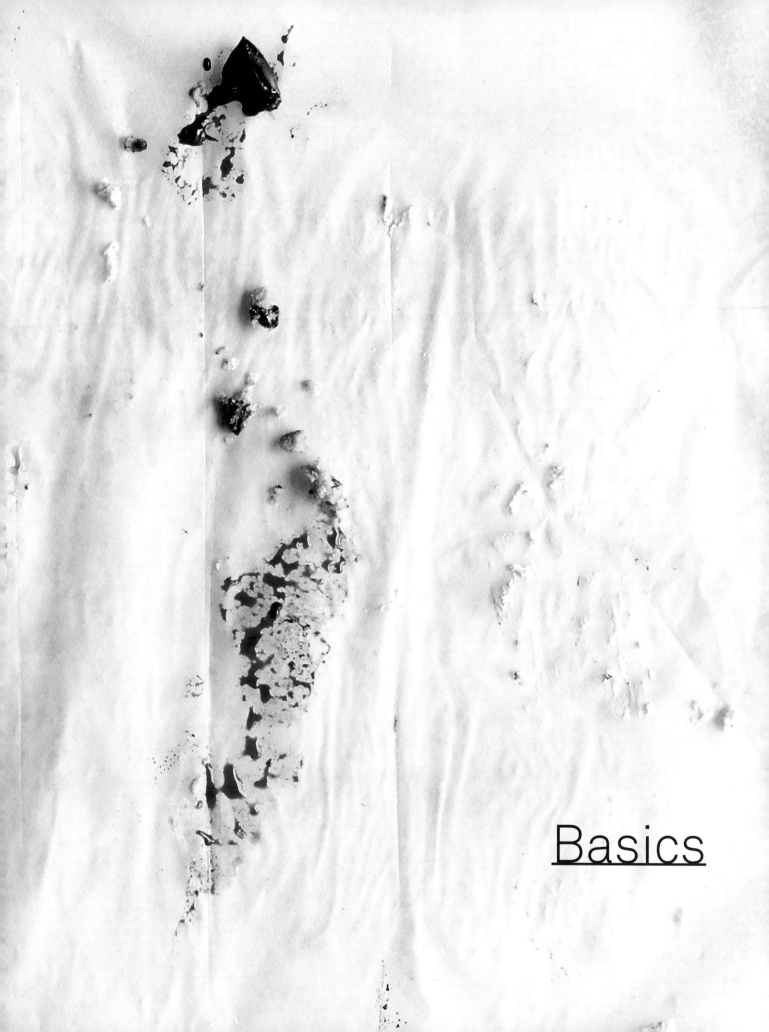

Basics

This apple sauce is used in a number of recipes. It helps to add bulk to recipes that have had the cane sugar removed, as well as providing its natural sweetness and fibre.

Apple purée

Makes 600 g (1 lb 5 oz/2 cups)
Gluten free

4 large apples (about 800 g/1 lb 12 oz)

Peel, core and roughly chop the apples. Put the apples and a splash of water in a medium saucepan over medium-low heat. Cover and cook, stirring occasionally, for 8–10 minutes or until tender. Stir and mash the apples, still over the heat, until broken down – they should be mushy and quite thick.

Remove from the heat and set aside to cool.

It is fine to have a little bit of texture, but if you prefer a smooth sauce, whiz in a food processor or use a hand-held blender and purée until smooth.

The purée will keep for 3–4 days in an airtight container in the refrigerator. It also freezes well for a couple of months – portion the purée into small containers or spoon into ice-cube trays, freeze and seal in an airtight container.

This fantastic jam is used in the Coconut raspberry jam slice (page 51) and the Jam duffins (page 53), but it is just as delicious simply spread on a slice of fresh bread. Make it with fresh berries when they are in season and plentiful, or use frozen berries any time of the year.

Raspberry chia jam

Makes: 420 g (15 oz/1½ cups)
Gluten free

500 g (1 lb 2 oz) fresh or frozen raspberries or mixed berries
2 tablespoons rice malt syrup
2 tablespoons freshly squeezed lemon juice
2 tablespoons chia seeds

Put the berries, rice malt syrup and lemon juice in a heavy-based saucepan over medium-low heat. Cook, stirring often, for about 30 minutes or until the berries are broken down and the mixture is slightly reduced and thickened. Remove from the heat and stir in the seeds. The mixture will thicken further as it cools.

Transfer to a clean airtight container. This jam will keep in the refrigerator for a couple of weeks.

A half-quantity of this recipe is enough to make the lid for a 24 cm (9½ in) pie or six cruffins (page 72). The slivers of butter that remain between the layers of dough give this pastry its flakiness. The yeast provides an extra lift, though it is not a traditional ingredient in rough puff. The pastry will keep for a few days in the refrigerator, or freezes for up to a month.

Rough puff pastry

Makes 1.2 kg (2 lb 10 oz)

500 g (1 lb 2 oz/3⅓ cups) plain bread or baker's flour, plus extra for dusting
2 teaspoons instant dried yeast
1 teaspoon salt
400 g (14 oz) butter, chilled and cut into 1 cm (½ in) pieces.
150 ml (5 fl oz) iced water
150 ml (5 fl oz) cold full cream (whole) milk

Mix the flour, yeast and salt together in a large bowl. Add the butter and toss through the flour with your fingers until coated. Add the water and milk, and mix and press the mixture together to form a rough dough, being careful to leave the butter in lumps. Do not knead.

On a clean work surface lightly dusted with flour, press the pastry into a square about 3 cm (1¼ in) thick. Roll it out to a rectangle about 20 cm x 40 cm (8 in x 15¾ in) in size (or 20 cm x 30 cm/8 in x 12 in if you are making a half-quantity). It will seem very messy but don't worry, it will all come together as the process continues.

Fold the dough in by thirds, as you would to fold a letter, brushing off any excess flour as you go. Rotate the dough 90 degrees and then repeat the rolling and folding instructions, using extra flour to stop the dough sticking, and to lightly coat any bits of butter that stick out. It will still look quite rough at this stage with visible lumps of butter, but it should look more like a dough now.

Wrap the dough well in plastic wrap and chill for 30 minutes in the refrigerator. Repeat the above process twice more. The dough is ready to use after it has been chilled three times. The finished dough should be smooth and elastic, with fine slivers of butter between the layers of dough. If you cut through the dough with a sharp knife, you will see the layers quite clearly.

This dough will keep for 2–3 days, well-wrapped in plastic wrap in the refrigerator. It can also be frozen for 3–4 weeks. Thaw in the refrigerator for several hours before use.

It's possible to make rough puff pastry with gluten-free flour, although it does require some patience! Keep a careful eye on the patches of butter – ensure that they are always dusted with a little more flour to keep them from bursting through your slowly developing dough. The slivers of butter that remain between the layers of dough give this pastry its flakiness and lift.

Gluten-free rough puff pastry

Makes 600 g (1 lb 5 oz)
Gluten free

250 g (9 oz/1⅔ cup) gluten-free plain (all-purpose) flour, plus extra to dust
1 teaspoon xanthan gum
½ teaspoon salt
200 g (7 oz) butter, chilled and cut into 1 cm (½ in) pieces
80 ml (2½ fl oz/⅓ cup) iced water
80 ml (2½ fl oz/⅓ cup) cold full cream (whole) milk

Mix the flour, xanthan gum and salt together in a large bowl. Add the butter and toss through the flour with your fingers until coated. Add the water and milk and mix. Press the mixture together to form a very rough dough, being careful to leave the butter in lumps. Add a little more water if you need to, just to bring the dough together. Do not knead.

On a clean work surface lightly dusted with flour, press the pastry into a square about 3 cm (1¼ in) thick. Roll it out to a rectangle 20 cm x 30 cm (8 in x 12 in) in size, ensuring that any patches of butter are dusted with a little more flour before they become exposed. It will seem very messy but don't worry, it will all come together. If you've made regular rough puff pastry before, you will note that this is a slower process with the gluten-free flour.

Fold the dough in by thirds, as you would to fold a letter, brushing off any excess flour as you go. Rotate the dough 90 degrees and then repeat the rolling and folding instructions, using extra flour to stop the dough sticking, and to lightly coat any bits of butter that stick out. It will still look quite rough at this stage with visible lumps of butter, but it should look more like a dough now.

Wrap the dough well in plastic wrap and chill for 30 minutes in the refrigerator. Repeat the above process twice more. The dough is ready to use after it has been chilled three times. The finished dough should be smooth and elastic, with fine slivers of butter between the layers of dough. If you cut through the dough with a sharp knife, you will see the layers quite clearly.

This dough will keep for 2–3 days, well-wrapped in plastic wrap in the refrigerator. It can also be frozen for 3–4 weeks. Thaw in the refrigerator for several hours before use.

This is a delicious and versatile frosting. Use the finest dextrose you can find (brands vary). If you think it may be a bit coarse, blend in a food processor (but don't lift the lid too quickly or you'll be covered in dextrose dust!) until you have an icing (confectioners') sugar consistency.

Lemon cream-cheese frosting

Makes 550 g (1 lb 3 oz/2½ cups)
Gluten free

250 g (9 oz) cream cheese, softened
finely grated zest of 1 lemon
125 g (4½ oz) butter, chopped into cubes and softened
1 tablespoon freshly squeezed lemon juice
160 g (5½ oz/1 cup) dextrose

Beat the cream cheese and lemon zest with an electric mixer until smooth. Add the butter 4–5 cubes at a time and beat until light and fluffy. Add all of the lemon juice and the dextrose a few spoonfuls at a time, and beat until well combined.

Use straight away, or store in the refrigerator in an airtight container for 2–3 days. Before use, bring back to room temperature and re-beat until smooth and creamy.

This deliciously moreish frosting can be used on cakes, cupcakes or used as a filling for crunchy biscuits.

Peanut butter frosting

Makes about 1 kg (2 lb 3 oz/5⅓ cups)
Gluten free

375 g (13 oz) butter, softened
420 g (15 oz/1½ cups) natural smooth peanut butter
120 g (4 oz/¾ cup) dextrose
100 g (3½ oz) sour cream

Beat the butter and peanut butter in a large bowl with an electric mixer, until light and fluffy. Add the dextrose gradually, beating well between each addition. Add the sour cream and beat until combined. Refrigerate to keep cool if the room temperature is warm.

This buttercream is delicious and so beautiful to work with. I like to use a small offset spatula to apply my icing — it makes the job so much easier. It is important that the butter is slightly softened as you beat it into the meringue mixture — it should be just soft enough to leave a dent from your fingertip when lightly pressed.

Swiss meringue buttercream

Makes 1.5 kg (3 lb 5 oz/about 9 cups)

300 g (10½ oz) egg white (from about 9 eggs)
520 g (1 lb 2 oz/3¼ cups) dextrose
700 g (1 lb 9 oz) butter, cut into cubes and slightly softened (it should be
    soft enough to leave a dent from your finger when lightly pressed)
1 tablespoon natural vanilla extract

Put the egg white and dextrose in a large heatproof bowl. Place the bowl over a saucepan of simmering water (the bowl shouldn't touch the water) and whisk until the dextrose dissolves and the egg whites are quite warm. Test this by rubbing a little of the mixture between your thumb and forefinger — the mixture should be smooth, not grainy.

Beat the egg white mixture with an electric mixer on medium-high speed until you have a meringue that is thick and glossy, and the side of the bowl is at room temperature when you touch it. This will take about 10 minutes, depending on your mixer.

With the mixer on medium speed, add the cubes of butter gradually, beating well between each addition, until the meringue is silky smooth. You may find that the mixture will separate and curdle at some point in the mixing process — do not panic, if you keep beating it should come back together. If the room temperature is too warm (around 18°C/64°F is ideal) and the mixture seems quite soft, pop the bowl in the refrigerator for 10–15 minutes to cool it down.

Add the vanilla and beat on low speed until combined.

Use straight away, or store in the refrigerator in an airtight container, for up to a week. Before use, bring the buttercream back to room temperature and re-beat until smooth and creamy. Beat in a little more softened butter if the mixture seems to curdle — it should come back together.

A

Almond bread 20

Almond mandarin cake 91

Almond pastry crust 143, 153

almond, coconut & chia cookies, Toasted 40

Almond, mandarin & orange blossom madeleines 84

Almond, rosewater & chocolate donut cakes 59

apple & cream cheese muffins, Spiced 71

apple pie, Rhubarb & 140

Apple purée 162

apples & pears, Orange blossom-baked 148

B

Baked kaffir lime & coconut rice pudding 159

Baked lemon cheesecake 115

Baked vanilla & pea donuts 64

banana & pear loaf, Seeded 100

Banana cashew cream 33

Banana chai blondies 47

Banana cream cheese frosting 133

bars, Superfood 56

Beetroot chocolate brownies 52

biscotti, Rosemary, hazelnut & orange 36

Biscuits & cookies

Almond bread 20

Brown butter pecan shortbread fingers 24

Cacao nib hazelnut cookies 19

Carrot cake biscuits 27

Chewy oat cookies 32

Chocolate shortbread sandwich biscuits with banana cashew cream 33

Cracked pepper biscuits 16

Crunchy lemon & polenta shortbread flowers 15

Ginger biscuits 12

Passionfruit cashew cream melting moments 28

Peanut butter cookies 21

Roasted cocoa crackle cookies 31

Rosemary, hazelnut & orange biscotti 36

Tahini shortbread buttons 39

Toasted almond, coconut & chia cookies 40

blondies, Banana chai 47

Brown butter frosting 107

Brown butter loaf with brown butter frosting 107

Brown butter pecan shortbread fingers 24

Brownies with coconut–date swirl 44

brownies, Beetroot chocolate 52

buttercream, Swiss meringue 167

C

Cacao nib hazelnut cookies 19

cake pops, Matcha 126

cake, Sweet potato, lime & poppy seed 92

Caramelised seeds 76

Carrot cake biscuits 27

Carrot cake with lemon cream cheese frosting 122

Carrot, parsnip & cardamom loaf 104

cashew cream, Banana 33

cashew cream, Passionfruit 28

chai blondies, Banana 47

Chai chia cupcakes 63

cheesecake tart, Lime 112

cheesecake, Baked lemon 115

cheesecake, Cookies & cream blueberry 109

cheesecake, Peanut butter swirl 108

cheesecake, Ricotta, fig & hazelnut 116

Chewy oat cookies 32

Choc avocado choux puffs 76

Choc avocado mousse 76

chocolate brownies, Beetroot 52

Chocolate cake 88

chocolate cake, Everyday 96

Chocolate crème pâtissière 130

Chocolate drizzle 125

Chocolate glaze 59

Chocolate icing 96

Chocolate layer cake with peanut butter frosting 125

Chocolate pear frangipane galettes 83

Chocolate shortbread sandwich biscuits with banana cashew cream 33

Chocolate, beetroot and orange cupcakes 60

Chocolate, pistachio & cardamom scones 68

Chocolaty sweet potato & macadamia cream cake 119

Choux puff mixture 76

Cinnamon powder 53

Cinnamon, apple & cream cheese scrolls 80

cocoa crackle cookies, Roasted 31

coconut & chia cookies, Toasted almond, 40

Coconut & pandan crème brûlée 156

Coconut cake with lime syrup 97

Coconut matcha cake with matcha cake pops 126

Coconut raspberry jam slice 51

Coconut Swiss meringue buttercream 126

Cookies & cream blueberry cheesecake 109

Cookies, see Biscuits & cookies

Cracked pepper biscuits 16

cream cheese frosting, Lemon 166

Creamy raspberry & orange tart 153

crème brûlée, Coconut & pandan 156

crème pâtissière, Chocolate 130

Crispy crumble topping 152

Croquembouche 130

cruffins, Earl grey & fig 72

Crumble topping 145

crumble, Peach, nectarine & ginger 145

crumble, Rhubarb & strawberry crispy 152

Crunchy lemon & polenta shortbread flowers 15

cupcakes, Chai chia 63

cupcakes, Chocolate, beetroot and orange 60

D

donut cakes, Almond, rosewater & chocolate 59

donuts, Baked vanilla & pea 64

donuts, Spiced pumpkin 65

duffins, Jam 53

E

Earl grey & fig cruffins 72

Everyday chocolate cake 96

F

Fig, prune & cranberry crumble slice 48

food colours, Natural 137

Frangipane 83

frosting, Banana cream cheese 133

frosting, Brown butter 107

frosting, Lemon cream-cheese 166

frosting, Peanut butter 166

fruit buns, Sticky 75

G

galettes, Chocolate pear frangipane 83

Ginger biscuits 12

Gluten-free rough puff pastry 165

H

hazelnut cookies, Cacao nib 19

Hazelnut, rose & orange cake with roasted strawberries & whipped ricotta 129

Hummingbird cake 95

Hummingbird layer cake with pineapple flowers 133

I,J

icing, Lime 63

Jam duffins 53

jam, Raspberry chia 163

L

Labne 153

lemon cheesecake, Baked 115

Lemon cream-cheese frosting 166

Lemon tart 143

Lime cheesecake tart 112

Lime icing 63

Lime syrup 97

loaf, Seeded banana & pear 100

M

macadamia cream cake, Chocolaty sweet potato & 119

Madeleines, Almond, mandarin & orange blossom 84

Mandarin & bay leaf olive oil loaf 103

mandarin cake, Almond 91

mascarpone topping, Orange 60

Matcha cake pops 126

melting moments, Passionfruit cashew cream 28

muffins, Spiced apple & cream cheese 71

O

oat cookies, Chewy 32

olive oil loaf, Mandarin & bay leaf 103

Orange blossom-baked apples & pears 148

Orange blossom, yoghurt & semolina cake 134

Orange mascarpone topping 60

P

Passionfruit cashew cream 28

Passionfruit cashew cream melting moments 28

Peach, nectarine & ginger crumble 145

Peanut brittle 125

Peanut butter cookies 21

Peanut butter frosting 166

Peanut butter swirl cheesecake 108

pears, Orange blossom-baked apples & 148

pie, Rhubarb & apple 140

pie, Roasted pumpkin 144

pineapple flowers, Hummingbird layer cake with 133

polenta shortbread flowers, Crunchy lemon & 15

poppy seed cake, Sweet potato, lime & 92

puff pastry, Gluten-free rough 165

puff pastry, Rough 164

Pumpkin & fennel scones 77

pumpkin pie, Roasted 144

R

Rainbow cake 137

Raspberry chia jam 163

Rhubarb & apple pie 140

Rhubarb & strawberry crispy crumble 152

rice pudding, Baked kaffir lime & coconut 159

Ricotta, fig & hazelnut cheesecake 116

Roasted cocoa crackle cookies 31

Roasted pumpkin pie 144

Rosemary, hazelnut & orange biscotti 36

Rough puff pastry 164

rough puff pastry, Gluten-free 165

S

scones, Chocolate, pistachio & cardamom 68

scones, Pumpkin & fennel 77

scrolls, Cinnamon, apple & cream cheese 80

Seeded banana & pear loaf 100

semolina cake, Orange blossom, yoghurt & 134

shortbread buttons, Tahini 39

shortbread fingers, Brown butter pecan 24

shortbread flowers, Crunchy lemon & polenta 15

shortbread sandwich biscuits with banana cashew cream, Chocolate 33

slice, Coconut raspberry jam 51

slice, Fig, prune & cranberry crumble 48

Spiced apple & cream cheese muffins 71

Spiced pumpkin donuts 65

Sticky fruit buns 75

strawberry crispy crumble, Rhubarb & 152

Superfood bars 56

Sweet potato, lime & poppy seed cake 92

Swiss meringue buttercream 167

T

Tahini shortbread buttons 39

tart, Creamy raspberry & orange 153

tart, Lemon 143

Tarte Tatin 151

Toasted almond, coconut & chia cookies 40

Toffee 130

GLUTEN-FREE RECIPES

Almond mandarin cake 91

almond, coconut & chia cookies, Toasted 40

Almond, mandarin & orange blossom madeleines 84

Almond, rosewater & chocolate donut cakes 59

apple pie, Rhubarb & 140

apples & pears, Orange blossom-baked 148

Baked kaffir lime & coconut rice pudding 159

Baked lemon cheesecake 115

Banana chai blondies 47

blondies, Banana chai 47

Brownies with coconut–date swirl 44

Cacao nib hazelnut cookies 19

Carrot cake biscuits 27

Carrot, parsnip & cardamom loaf 104

chai blondies, Banana 47

Chai chia cupcakes 63

cheesecake tart, Lime 112

cheesecake, Baked lemon 115

cheesecake, Cookies & cream blueberry 109

cheesecake, Peanut butter swirl 108

Chocolate cake 88

Chocolate pear frangipane galettes 83

Chocolate, beetroot and orange cupcakes 60

Chocolate, pistachio & cardamom

scones 68

Chocolaty sweet potato & macadamia cream cake 119

coconut & chia cookies, Toasted almond, 40

Coconut & pandan crème brûlée 156

Coconut raspberry jam slice 51

Cookies & cream blueberry cheesecake 109

Creamy raspberry & orange tart 153

crème brûlée, Coconut & pandan 156

crumble, Peach, nectarine & ginger 145

cupcakes, Chai chia 63

cupcakes, Chocolate, beetroot and orange 60

donut cakes, Almond, rosewater & chocolate 59

galettes, Chocolate pear frangipane 83

hazelnut cookies, Cacao nib 19

Hazelnut, rose & orange cake with roasted strawberries & whipped ricotta 129

lemon cheesecake, Baked 115

Lemon tart 143

Lime cheesecake tart 112

macadamia cream cake, Chocolaty sweet potato & 119

Madeleines, Almond, mandarin & orange blossom 84

mandarin cake, Almond 91

Orange blossom-baked apples & pears 148

pastry, Gluten-free rough puff 165

Peach, nectarine & ginger crumble 145

Peanut butter cookies 21

Peanut butter swirl cheesecake 108

pears, Orange blossom-baked apples & 148

pie, Rhubarb & apple 140

pie, Roasted pumpkin 144

pumpkin pie, Roasted 144

Rhubarb & apple pie 140

rice pudding, Baked kaffir lime & coconut 159

Roasted pumpkin pie 144

rough puff pastry, Gluten-free 165

scones, Chocolate, pistachio & cardamom 68

shortbread buttons, Tahini 39

slice, Coconut raspberry jam 51

Tahini shortbread buttons 39

tart, Creamy raspberry & orange 153

tart, Lemon 143

Toasted almond, coconut & chia cookies 40

Acknowledgements

To the fabulous Paul McNally: thank you so much for your vision and the opportunity to work with you and Smith Street Books to produce this beautiful book. It has been a whirlwind and a blast. Also, thank you to Lucy Heaver and Hannah Koelmeyer for your precision and editing expertise.

Big thanks to the dynamic, talented shoot team: Chris Middleton for the beautiful images and Vicki Valsamis for your styling skill, creative eye, meticulous planning and for going above and beyond for every shot. There would have been nothing to shoot if it weren't for the gorgeous Jemima Good – for all your hard work, keeping things moving in the kitchen, your food skills and for keeping me sane, thank you.

Thanks and love to family, friends and neighbours for taste-testing along the way (and over the years), and for your valuable feedback.

I would not be able to create and spend my time doing what I love without the incredible sacrifice and support of my wonderful husband Kaine. You keep our world turning and on track. You, with our beautiful boys are the greatest. I love you and thank you for putting up with me (and my noisy mixer).

There are not enough words to express the thanks I owe to my amazing mum Doreen, and my late dad Alan. Thank you for your tireless support and confidence in me from the very beginning, from way back when Nanna taught me to make her legendary scones at her apron strings.

About the author

Caroline Griffiths is a qualified home economist, cook, food writer and food stylist with a keen interest in nutrition. She is a passionate food expert with over 25 years of food industry experience, having worked in Australia's best known test kitchens, including the *Australian Women's Weekly*. She has contributed to many cookbooks, food magazines and websites. Caroline loves to create recipes that are flavourful, wholesome, creative and achievable.

Published in 2016 by Smith Street Books
Melbourne | Australia
smithstreetbooks.com

ISBN: 978-1-925418-04-0

CIP data is available from the National Library of Australia

Publisher: Paul McNally
Senior Editor: Lucy Heaver
Designer: Ava Strack
Photographer: Chris Middleton
Stylist: Vicki Valsamis
Food preparation: Caroline Griffiths
Food assistant: Jemima Good

The publisher would like to thank The Establishment Studios, Melbourne, for the use of the props and surfaces used throughout this book.

Colour reproduction by Splitting Image Colour Studio
Printed & bound in China by C&C Offset Printing Co., Ltd.

Book 4
10 9 8 7 6 5 4 3